MOTHERLAND

MOTHERLAND

*The Disintegration of a Family in a
Collapsed Venezuela*

A MEMOIR

PAULA RAMÓN

WITH TRANSLATIONS BY JULIA SANCHES AND JENNIFER SHYUE

Previously published as *Mãe pátria: A desintegração de uma família na Venezuela em
colapso* by Companhia das Letras in Brazil in 2020. Translated from Portuguese by Julia
Sanches and Jennifer Shyue. First published in English by Amazon Crossing in 2023.

Published by Amazon Crossing, Seattle

www.apub.com

Amazon, the Amazon logo, and Amazon Crossing are trademarks of Amazon.com,
Inc., or its affiliates.

ISBN-13: 9781542036900 (hardcover)
ISBN-13: 9781542036917 (paperback)
ISBN-13: 9781542036894 (digital)

Cover design by David Drummond

Unless otherwise noted, images are courtesy of the author. Oil rig © José Isaac Bula
Urrutia/Alamy Stock Photo; tunnel view of Caracas, Venezuela © apomares/Getty
Images; sunset over Caracas, Venezuela © Douglas Olivares/Shutterstock

Printed in the United States of America

First edition

To Paulina and Jesús

Contents

AUTHOR'S NOTE

This is my story, and that of my family, as I remember it. It is my personal effort to reconstruct painful episodes that scarred my life. Some words are extracted from real emails or messages, and some names have been changed for privacy reasons. Most of the references to Venezuela's sociopolitical turmoil have been verified using news articles and documents, but some of the more contemporary references are common knowledge. There are things that only those of us who have been through them truly know.

Introduction

A Path of No Return

I grew up in a place where rules were made to be broken. My country took pride in its main social asset, "criollo clever," or the belief that we could outsmart everyone else. In a system that functioned according to long-established social codes, we quickly learned that when a public employee claimed something was difficult, what they wanted was a bribe, and that getting anything done required a friend, or a friend of a friend, to call in a favor. I was raised to play the game, but even though my mother taught me to duck and weave, eventually Venezuela brought me to my knees.

In the 1970s, my hometown, Maracaibo, and its enormous oil reserves were a symbol of the future in what was then the most prosperous country in the Caribbean. It was a vibrant era for the country owing to the explosion in the price of oil, which spilled ceaselessly from our soil. In a continent that staggered between soldiers, saviors, and economic crises, Venezuela was a model for democracy.

It was in those years of euphoria that my parents met in Maracaibo. Neither of them was from there, but after a chance encounter they embraced that place, hot as an ember, and worked to put down roots together. My parents knew the bitterness of exile, and I grew up hearing their stories: Papá had survived two wars and a concentration camp; Mamá had rebuilt her life hundreds of kilometers away from her hometown after a childhood of poverty. Now that I think about it, maybe that's why ever since I was little, I've felt the need to hold on to things, to belong somewhere.

My parents built their life together against the backdrop of Venezuela's wild ups and downs, but their financial approaches could not have been more different. In the affluent years, Papá lived in hotels, wore expensive suits, and dined in restaurants. Meanwhile, Mamá—who didn't even open the menu when my father took her out because she always ordered the cheapest dish, arroz a la cubana—saved for the future. That's why, after the petroleum party gave way to the lean years and the hangover began for a country whose future was no longer promising, my father had nothing and my mother owned the house where they would raise their family, and where I was born in 1981.

When I was a child, Mamá drew on her creativity and thriftiness as the country's economic and social indicators deteriorated. Because of her resilience and determination, and my father's willingness to work ever harder without complaint—even as he grew older in those years of social unrest, violence, inflation, and depreciation—my brothers and I felt we lacked for nothing. I had been born into and raised in a crisis, but my experience of crisis was softened by my parents' hard work. And I believed things couldn't get worse, that it was only up from there.

Starting when I was small, my mother instilled in me the idea that education was the only way up the social ladder. That attitude wasn't a common one in a country grounded in magic formulas. Besides oil, the winning ticket for many Venezuelan parents came out of baseball or beauty contests. Though Mamá never ruled out her little one walking on the country's most important stage, she left nothing to chance. She was determined to do whatever it took for me to follow in her footsteps and go to college.

By the time I turned twelve, I had lived through as many coups as presidential elections. When I started high school in the 1990s, Venezuela was experiencing one turbulent stretch after another. During the chaos, Venezuelans came to embrace anti-politics and a new savior whose promises of revindication gave them hope.

I began studying journalism around the time that Hugo Chávez—a charismatic, young former soldier who'd led a coup six years earlier—won the presidential election. At the time, I never could have imagined that my family and I were about to start down a path of no return.

More than twenty years of "Bolivarian Revolution" have passed since December 6, 1998, when Hugo Chávez announced the birth of "a new nation" to a crowd in Caracas on the night of his election. Contrary to his promises, "El Comandante" and his project didn't decrease inequality in Venezuela. Instead, inequality rose with the creation of an elite class that grew prosperous by illicit means. Far from fighting corruption, the government made corruption one of the most booming businesses in the country. Rather than reducing the rates of violence, the government denied the numbers, gave the armed forces and law enforcement leeway to assert their authority as they wished, and formed new groups that enacted their own approaches to repression and social control. Today, the revolution is sustained through the explicit support of these groups. By endorsing the revolution to keep up their own small privileges, they wring out a nation in tatters.

I spent years as a journalist covering the marches of the "red tide" that would routinely fill whole avenues in the heart of Caracas, tricolor flags fluttering overhead. People's emotions rode high, to the point of tears. I remember how excited Mamá was as she watched Chávez make speeches promising a new era. Nothing is left of those years but videos that the state media—now simply the government's propaganda apparatus—loop endlessly in a bid to encapsulate the past. The images show flags, soldiers, and other scenes of empty patriotism woven from rhetorical acrobatics that lionize the revolution—a revolution that imprisons dissidents, silences voices, and distorts any whiff of democracy for the sake of staying in power forever, by any means necessary.

I left Venezuela in 2010, shortly before the end of another oil boom that fed Chávez's hunger for power. Though my mother and I didn't see eye to eye on most things, we were close, and in the years that followed, we would have to confront the difficulties of physical distance. It wasn't just a matter of finding ways to talk and see each other while being thousands of kilometers apart. As the country collapsed, so did our entire family.

I went back to Venezuela every year, only to realize once more that the country I'd grown up in no longer existed. I watched as the gap between me and my brothers grew wider and Mamá slowly slipped out of my hands, no matter how hard I tried to hold on.

She had taught me how to mend, wash, and cook, driven by a relentless obsession with preparing me for life. "One day I won't be here anymore," she'd say, making my heart beat faster at the memory of my father's death when I was twelve. Through the years, Mamá equipped me with a handbook of life lessons and tricks. But these stopped working as the country's tragic circumstances deepened.

At some point, our relationship became a jumble of accounts, transfers, bureaucratic red tape, and logistical negotiations. And one day, despite how tightly I'd held on and how hard she'd fought, she closed her eyes and let go of the chaos. I never learned the cause of her death and have no way of finding out. Yet another thing my country took from me. I know she didn't suffer; I know because I was on the other end of the phone when it happened. For years, I'd lived in fear of hearing the phone ring and having to face the bearer of bad news. When the time came, it happened in a way I couldn't have imagined. Nothing was like I expected. All that's left of the Venezuela I knew and the family I was born into are memories.

I often dream about her. In my dreams she isn't sitting in the wheelchair she came to depend on in her final years; she's standing, her jet-black hair falling to her shoulders. *I know I'm dreaming,* I say to her, and then I start to sob. I wake up crying tears made more bitter by the fact that all I want is to go back to sleep so I can see and talk to her. This recurring dream replaced the one I used to have when my mother was alive, where burglars would break into her house. I would try and fail to protect her. I always woke up when the burglars—who were always faceless—were just about to reach her.

The last time I visited Maracaibo was in March 2019, four months after her wake. Walking through that city on the western edge of the country was like walking among the ruins of my childhood and the old promises of wealth and national prosperity. The city's disintegration was precipitous; it was as if a decade of destruction had occurred in the space of a year.

Dozens of food shortages throughout the years had tipped thousands of people into hunger, but by 2019 food was starting to hit shelves. Earlier that year, several of Maracaibo's largest stores had been stripped bare by mobs of people; driven by the need for catharsis, they had sacked everything in their path. A power failure that March had left almost the entire country without electricity for days. Without electricity, the water also stopped running. Staying hydrated in a city where temperatures exceed 85 degrees Fahrenheit became a luxury.

My mother's house was still intact, even if it was totally different from how I remembered it as a child. Like a time capsule, it stored our memories, laughter, and fights. This was my first time walking into that space without her there. There were no snacks, no coffee, no "Hi, sweetie." My mother's home was just an empty house in a country that was slowly emptying out. As I walked inside, I thought about Miguel Otero Silva's 1955 novel *Casas muertas* (*Dead Houses*), which is about Ortiz, a Venezuelan town on the plains that has been leveled by malaria.

A dead house, among a thousand dead houses, muttering the hopeless messages of a bygone era. Everyone in the town talked about those days. The grandparents had lived through them, the parents had witnessed how everything collapsed, the children had been raised between stories and yearning. Nowhere else, never before, had people lived the past the way it was lived in that town on the plains. There was nothing to look forward to but fever, death, and the guinea grass of the cemetery. Looking into the past was different.

More than six decades after that novel was published, as the country grew ever more dilapidated, Otero Silva's story still had a prescient ring; the absences and my yearning filled me with inconsolable sadness.

Suddenly, as I stood looking into the front hallway, I saw how everything had changed. Thirty years earlier, my parents had thrown parties in this house, which was now barricaded with layers of security gates. The emptiness hurt as much as everything we had turned into. The crisis we faced had stolen years from us and turned our houses into bunkers, our routines into logistics operations. The plants Mamá had cultivated with such determination continued to flower. In some ways, the house felt like an extension of her, those plants the only living thing left of her after all those years.

I didn't know it then, but that was the last time I would visit the city and enter that house, the last time I would see those plants. One of my brothers obtained an expropriation order that allowed him to take ownership of the property and the house, arguing that I didn't live in the country. I didn't fight him on it. In some ways, it felt liberating; none of it was my responsibility anymore, and Venezuela was a distant memory.

I started writing this book a few days after my mother's funeral. These pages capture how I remember the last decades. They have given me an opportunity to reflect on what we went through as a family and as a country, a luxury I couldn't afford when my mother was alive. Although our country was not at war with anyone, millions of

Venezuelans were thrust into circumstances that resembled my dad's wartime memories. It brought out the worst in all of us. After decades of abundance, food and money became obsessions, breaking families apart and sending thousands of people out of the country in search of a better life.

Without my realizing it, during my time away from Venezuela, my parents—who had always been my home—had become my homeland. When Mamá died, the umbilical cord tethering me to her and to the terra-cotta floor of our house was suddenly severed. My grief was twofold, and it grew into an emotional and geographical void one could call rootlessness. Writing about it ultimately exorcized my feelings. Like Tita in *Like Water for Chocolate*, whose tears soaked into her cooking and generated emotions in her guests, my mourning floods these pages, which have become a letter of farewell to my parents and my country. The only time I get to see them again is in my dreams.

Chapter 1

The Golden Years

When my father, Jesús, arrived in Venezuela by ship in 1947, penniless and carrying only his trauma, he was dazzled by the colors of the Caribbean and by the prosperity of a country that felt distant from the wars and concentration camps he'd left behind in Europe. Venezuela seemed to move to a different rhythm.

He was born in 1920 in Letur, a small town with whitewashed houses and narrow corridors, bathed by a river. From afar, tucked between the mountains of southern Spain, it looks like a brown fortress in the middle of groves of olives trees. The Spanish Civil War burst into his life when he was just a teenager, and since his was a communist family, he put on his uniform and went with Juan, an older brother, to the battlefront to defend the republic. They never returned to their hometown.

At some point between 1937 and 1939, my father and his brother—like thousands of Spanish fighters—fled to France, where another war awaited them. When I was a child, Papá told me how during World War II, he volunteered to fight the German army on the western front, convinced it was his duty. His brother, already injured, stayed in France. Eight decades later, I would find a photo of the brothers taken just before they said goodbye and my father went off to war once more. They never saw each other again.

My father was captured at the front in 1940 and sent to a POW camp in northeastern Germany. Defending the republic during the Spanish Civil War came with a cost. My dad, as well as thousands of Spaniards in his same situation, were declared stateless by Francisco Franco's government, which turned them into pariahs and put them in limbo. As they were no longer considered prisoners of war, Germany sent them to concentration camps. In June 1941, my father arrived at Mauthausen concentration camp, built on a hill in a small town in occupied Austria, where he became number 3431 and survived four horrifying years until the end of the war.

When he was released, he couldn't go back to Spain, which was still under Franco's rule. He wasn't a citizen of any other country and had no place to go, so he stayed in Paris and started a new life as a carpenter, a job he'd embraced as a survival strategy in Mauthausen.

Shortly after, he married a Spanish woman in the French capital and they had their first son. According to a friend's testimony that I read years later, as Papá went on living life in Paris, he kept hearing about a place called Venezuela, where wells spurted endless streams of oil, attracting international companies and creating the need for labor in this industry and others. A country that had just elected a novelist, Rómulo Gallegos, in its first free elections and signed an agreement to receive and settle migrants from tattered Europe. Eventually he convinced his wife and her family to leave the little bit of stability they'd managed to achieve in postwar France and venture to that tropical land of abundance.

They traveled by ship as political refugees with the promise of a warm welcome from Venezuela's burgeoning democracy, which was ruled by a government that had placed immigration at the center of its country's development.

But after the wars and dictatorships that punctuated the nineteenth century and the turn of the twentieth century, Venezuela wasn't ready for democracy. In November 1948, just before my father's arrival, a coup deposed Gallegos's government and installed a military junta that would continue receiving immigrants from Europe but view Spanish leftists with suspicion.

For more than a month my father and his family were forced to stay in a camp for immigrants on the coast of Venezuela, not far from where they disembarked. Eventually, friends of his father-in-law helped get them released, and the family settled in Caracas.

The junta remained in power for a decade, with General Marcos Pérez Jiménez presiding most of those years. He clashed with dissidents, many of them from Gallegos's party—the social-democratic party Democratic Action—and won support from constituents who sought a conservative leader.

My father was not one of those supporters. He embraced the social democratic cause as his own and contributed by performing small tasks for the party, whose top leaders were in exile. But even under the political circumstances, he was able to start a new life. He was naturalized as Venezuelan and started working right away.

In Caracas, Papá got used to being called "musiú," a term derived from "monsieur," which was how Venezuelans referred to all the Europeans who came in the postwar waves.

The war apparently receded in his memory as he moved from a life of poverty in Europe to the upper-middle class in Venezuela, which lauded him for being European and white. He lived in a neighborhood full of cafés and Spanish taverns, at the foot of El Ávila—the mountains that frame the Caracas valley and separate the capital from the Caribbean Sea—and cooking became one of his great pleasures. Years later, when I told his family in Letur about the delicious squid and paella he used to make, his nephew noted that my father's familiarity with Spanish dishes was impressive, given that he had often gone hungry in the Spain of his youth.

Papá never had a specific profession, though he was always dabbling in different businesses.

With the influx of oil income, Pérez Jiménez promoted his "New National Ideal," a conservative attempt to modernize the country by constructing spectacular buildings and hundreds of kilometers of highway.

One of his signature projects was a building complex erected in the center of Caracas to address the housing crisis that had developed as migrants continued moving to the city. Pérez Jiménez's administration devised a residential park made up of several blocks—inspired by the Swiss-French architect Le Corbusier's Unité d'habitation—in an effort to get rid of the shanties cropping up on Ávila's mountainsides.

That development near the presidential palace would become the national epicenter of transformation and social struggle for the next few decades. After Pérez Jiménez was ousted in 1958, the complex was named 23 de Enero to honor the day Venezuela turned once more toward democracy.

That year, Democratic Action, its archrival COPEI (the Social Christian Party), and the centrist Democratic Republican Union shook hands on the Punto Fijo Pact, whose goal was to guarantee the country's governability (and exclude the Communist Party). My father celebrated democracy by voting in his first presidential elections. Rómulo Betancourt came to power for his second term (he'd served a brief term before Gallegos), marking the start of an era my father would remember with happiness.

The period of political and economic transformation when my father began his new life in Venezuela also defined my mother's early years.

She was born in Capacho—a small town in the Venezuelan Andes less than an hour from the Colombian border—in August 1945, just a few days after my father got married in France. Her given name was Paulina, but everyone called her Paula.

My mother did not remember the short period when Rómulo Gallegos and Rómulo Betancourt tried to create a democratic Venezuela, drawing on the economic boon enabled by the vast oil fields discovered decades earlier in the western part of the country. She lived under Marcos Pérez Jiménez's military dictatorship for most of her childhood and grew up admiring men in uniform, convinced the country needed order and a firm hand to achieve progress.

Just like thousands of people who left behind farm work to seek their fortunes in the cities, lured by the legend of black gold, Mamá's older siblings moved the family when she was still a baby, from Capacho—where they'd made a living growing pineapples—to Táchira's state capital, San Cristóbal, where there were significantly more work opportunities. With an illiterate mother and an absent, alcoholic father, her siblings were the ones who gave structure to my mother's impoverished childhood.

In San Cristóbal, the brood woke up at dawn every day to grind corn for the arepas they sold on the street. On Christmas Eve, with no money for toys, they would stand at the entrance of the Círculo Militar, where the city's elite celebrated the holidays, in hope of receiving a gift from one of the powerful men in uniform.

By the time the dictatorship fell in 1958, my mother's older siblings had established their own food and clothing businesses. A few years later, her sister Marga decided to go to university in Maracaibo, a wellspring of oil north of the Andes. While most of the older siblings hadn't had access to school, it became an option for the younger ones, who started attending classes. Mamá was three or four years behind most of the other students, but the public school system made it possible for her to get an education. For high school, she attended the prestigious Liceo Simón Bolívar, an institution she never tired of praising.

Because education helped my mother climb the social ladder, one of her proudest memories was working up the courage in her early twenties to study in Maracaibo, at the university where her sister Marga had become a professor. Later I'd learn that it wasn't so much a desire for education that drove my mother to Maracaibo; it was my uncle Daniel, who was trying to help her find purpose after she discovered that her then-fiancé—someone I'd known nothing about—had a wife and five kids.

Mamá and I talked a lot, and though she shared details of her past with me, she never said anything about that fiancé, or how their relationship ended. That story came to me through other sources and helped me understand why she insisted that I be financially independent and repeatedly warned me not to trust men; it also explained why she was so attached to Maracaibo, the city that had taken her in.

When Mamá talked about how she got into university, she didn't mention good grades or a competitive admissions process. All she said was that she'd gone to the school's administrative offices and argued that she had a right to be there because she came from a humble family and wanted badly to learn.

My mother was an example of what used to be possible in Venezuela. As the tenth of eleven children from a poor rural family, Paula had managed to get a spot studying biology at the public university in the country's second most important city.

It was the late 1960s, when Maracaibo was known as the Saudi Arabia of Venezuela. Zulia's state capital—hot, the sun scorching as soon as day broke—was expanding along the shores of the enormous lake with which it shares a name. An object of local pride, the lake was the region's largest freshwater reservoir. But beneath its surface, thousands of kilometers of pipeline pumped oil. With that oil came a distorted logic that to this day lurks in Venezuela's economy and the national psyche.

Venezuelans had come to believe in a false reality: that discovering oil had made them rich forever. They could now live comfortably off the rent from wells that yielded an ever-valuable resource. As a country, they'd won the lottery, and the government was in charge of administering the prize. The oil boom allowed it to put in place welfare and populist policies that led to a permanent state of illusion, one where it was possible to retire young, buy a house after a few years' work, have new cars every year, drink imported whiskey, and forget that gasoline could be expensive; for Venezuelans, it was practically free.

After my mother graduated from university in 1972, she started teaching at a public high school in a commuter town near Maracaibo. Shortly thereafter, a conflict that had nothing to do with Venezuela changed its fate. In response to the Yom Kippur War of October 1973—when a coalition led by Egypt and Syria attacked Israeli positions in the Golan Heights and the Sinai Peninsula—an embargo against countries supporting Israel caused the price of crude to skyrocket. By then, crude was Venezuela's main product, which was extremely good news: the country could profit from oil more than ever before.

My mother's life continued to improve, as did the lives of her siblings, the majority of them married and living in San Cristóbal or Maracaibo. When she thought back to the Christmases spent begging for a toy at the gates to the Círculo Militar, Mamá felt proud of how far she'd made it in life. "I was poor, but I got an education," she used to say whenever she lectured people. Given that my father's schooling was interrupted by the Spanish Civil War in 1936, I must have picked up my way of associating education with progress from Mamá.

By 1973, though things like TVs and record players were still luxuries beyond her reach, her teacher's salary had freed my mother from the habits of her university years, when she wore a homemade uniform to class, pretending to be a secretary because she didn't have the money to buy other clothes. To illustrate her point that studying led to immediate social mobility, my mom would bring up my aunt Elisa, who didn't go to school and was the only one in the brood to never buy a house, content to inherit the apartment the siblings eventually bought for my grandmother. "I would tell her, 'Elisa, go to college. Even if you don't learn anything, you could at least meet someone worthwhile,'" Mamá often said, not bothering to hide her low opinion of her brother-in-law.

With the advent of oil and the family's recently established ties to Maracaibo, which was six hours from San Cristóbal by highway, new patterns emerged in Mamá's family. Some siblings continued with their businesses, which were booming, but others veered off onto one of two trajectories. The men, engineers, aimed to build careers at the oil company, cinching lives filled with benefits. The women, teachers, went on the state's payroll, which gave them economic stability, health insurance, and flexible schedules to accommodate the children they'd go on to have.

While several countries in Latin America succumbed to harsh military dictatorships, Venezuela flourished, governed by what was in essence a rotation between Democratic Action and COPEI. The two parties' leaders enjoyed the country's seeming political and economic stability and grew complacent in power. Indeed, with its privileged geographic position—featuring mountains, the Amazon rain forest, and hundreds of kilometers of Caribbean shores—Venezuela appeared to have it all.

Mamá promised her votes to COPEI, the Social Christian Party also known as the Green Party, in part because she felt more of an affinity with them than she did with the social democratic principles of the "Adecos," as Democratic Action partisans were called. Even though she'd benefited from social policies all her life, she leaned right. She had this notion that some people deserved state support, while others did not. Still, if I had to sum up her ideology, I'd say that it was by and large pragmatic. The real reason she supported COPEI when she worked as a teacher was that she wanted to be transferred from her school in Ciudad Ojeda to one in Maracaibo, and the union leader, who belonged to COPEI, promised to make it happen. With a transfer, Mamá could finally stop commuting eighty kilometers to work every day.

It was on one of those exhausting journeys that she met my father. The year was 1974, and she was waiting at a stop for a "por puesto," one of a fleet of cars with a fixed route whose four seats went to paying passengers. Out of nowhere, my father stopped—smitten?—and offered her a ride. She refused at first, but then eventually gave in after the handsome fellow insisted. Later that day, she found him waiting outside the school at the end of her shift. That was Mamá's version of the story, which Papá, who was head over heels, never contradicted. Later I heard a different, somewhat less romantic version: Mamá and her friends were always asking for free rides, and my father simply happened to stop— just as anyone would have back then, when robbery, kidnapping, and homicide weren't everyday occurrences, and people, even strangers, were just people, not potential murderers. One thing's for sure: he did wait for her at the school's entrance.

Papá, who in different periods of his life ran a hardware store and a handful of small restaurants, was most economically successful when he held the now-extinct position of traveling salesman. He worked for an importer and would drive around the country offering products to clients. Jewelry, gadgets, watches—he was like a walking catalog. He spent more time on the road than at home in Caracas, with his wife and three children. He and his wife had been separated a few months before he met my mother. At least that's the story he told me, and I choose to believe it.

He was successful and attractive, and despite being twenty-five years older than Mamá, he was the finishing touch on her lofty dreams of social mobility, which featured a knight in shining armor who gave her pearls and her first TV set and took her out to restaurants she never would have ventured into on her own.

When they met, Papá was doing better financially than Mamá. Their age difference was probably the reason—after all, when he first arrived in oil-rich Venezuela, she was still a child.

While he lived in five-star hotels instead of buying a house, and upgraded to a new car every year, my mother saved with the goal of having a home of her own. Her older siblings in San Cristóbal had all started businesses and become parents. They owned houses, and one of them even had a small fleet of trucks. Her younger siblings in Maracaibo were still making their way, but things were very different compared to two decades earlier, when the clan would get up at dawn each day to mix arepas to sell. Now the siblings in both cities came up with reasons to meet every weekend and toss back imported whiskey.

In 1974, just as my parents began dating, one of the most charismatic politicians Venezuela has ever seen became president. Carlos Andrés Pérez was a social democrat. When oil prices abruptly increased, Pérez opted to nationalize the oil industry, indemnify the foreign companies that had been extracting oil from Venezuela's oil fields for decades, and create a legal framework that guaranteed the country's control over the industry's systems. A year later, Petróleos de Venezuela (PDVSA) was born. Suddenly, Venezuela was wealthier than ever.

Pérez capitalized on the bonanza, making his name synonymous with prosperity. He invested heavily in public spending, bolstering education and public health-care systems that were solid despite the fact that almost no taxes were collected. Venezuelans had purchasing power, unemployment was below 5 percent, and for many it was normal to travel to Miami to go on shopping sprees and buy Scotch. To this day, "That's cheap, give me two" is remembered as a popular Venezuelan refrain in Florida's stores. The city of Caracas, vibrant and cosmopolitan, was dubbed a "subsidiary of paradise." Pérez used part of the oil surplus to try to develop another economic hub in the eastern part of the country, where fast-flowing rivers and the discovery of mineral deposits foretold even more wealth for the invincible tropical paradise.

It was like money was growing on trees—or emerging from the bowels of the earth.

It was around then that my father, who never formally divorced his first wife, moved in with my mother, and children came onto the scene. My oldest brother, Luis, was born in 1976, and Andrés was born a year later. My mother was diagnosed soon after with arthritis and Sjögren's syndrome, a hereditary autoimmune disease that our city's doctors didn't know how to treat. The most conspicuous symptom was dryness of the mucous membranes. Annoyed that the politicians never kept their promise to transfer her job to Maracaibo, and held back by the limitations of her illnesses, Mamá retired after eight years of teaching, before she was even thirty-five. Once again, oil-rich Venezuela came to her aid, ensuring a full salary and free health care. After Papá moved in with Mamá, he left his traveling salesman job and became a family man. But he was still reluctant to buy a house, and my mom didn't want to live in hotels, so they compromised and rented an apartment for a few months. My mom's restraint couldn't have been more diametrically opposed to Papá's loose, bohemian approach to life, which perfectly suited the government of that era. He lived intensely, perhaps because there'd been so much death around him during the near decade of war he'd experienced as a young man in Europe. My mother lived cautiously, perhaps because there'd been so much poverty around her during her childhood in the Andes.

Not only did he not think about saving money or having a house to call his own, but also, in Mamá's words, "He lived outside of reality; he was a dreamer."

No longer a traveling salesman, my dad could now follow his dream—a dream that cost our family dearly. He decided to become a restaurateur. Mamá advised him to repeat the formula her brothers had followed: start small and invest part of the profits in growth. "But your father wanted to start big," my mother used to tell me, annoyed. Following the spirit of excess that marked the country at the time, Papá sank what little savings they had into various gastronomic adventures. And he failed again and again. This dream made it necessary for them to move a lot as well, between neighborhoods and even cities. Once, he decided to try his luck in San Cristóbal, where he spent the last of their savings on another culinary bet.

Papá's incessant business restarts and splurging left them vulnerable to any setback. At the tail end of the 1970s, a serious car accident sent him to the hospital. With Papá unable to work, Mamá put what money she had toward settling the restaurant's growing pile of unpaid bills. But it wasn't enough, and they had to close shop; they ended up broke, unable to pay the rent. Their landlord evicted Mamá along with my two brothers, then toddlers. Her siblings refused to take them in while Papá convalesced in the hospital. "They told me they would receive me with one of the boys, and suggested I leave my other baby at a care home while your dad recovered," she told me years later, half-angry, half-sad. So, thrust back into poverty, endlessly shuttling between the hospital and the kids, she made a decision that would torment her all her life: she left her two-year-old second son, Andrés, at the care home for a few days. Because of this, my brother harbored an eternal grudge against my mother, who, traumatized and driven by guilt, resolved to buy a house so her children would always have a place to call home.

"One day I got tired and decided to find a place to live," my mother later told me, as though her life were a screenplay where every situation was straightforward and every problem was easy to solve. That same day, she said, she found a two-story house with a gray stone facade in a commercial neighborhood flanked by two important avenues in a central area. With a down payment and a loan from the Ministry of Education, which despite my mother's precarious finances did not raise a single objection to her request, she bought the house that would become the focal point of our arguments and emotions throughout the next four decades.

According to my mother, the only thing a person needed to get what they wanted was determination. "You have to decide to do things," she'd say. I was raised—in the house she bought on her own—to believe this.

Those four walls were a testament to my mother's determination. Despite her intimate familiarity with poverty, she did not believe in socioeconomic inequality as a determining factor. But her story of prosperity was a product of the oil illusion in a country where the government managed so much money that a pensioner with no credit history could get a mortgage in a matter of days. When oil prices fell, the illusion came crashing down as swiftly as it had been built. Ultimately, my parents' prosperity, like the prosperity of so many at that time, turned out to be nothing more than a mirage made possible by oil.

Chapter 2

The Party's Over

By the start of the 1980s, my father had spent more than he could make—like the country—having burned through all his money in a bid to own a restaurant. All that was left of years of the high salary he earned as a traveling salesman were memories, watches, suits, and pearl necklaces from a bygone era. My mother had proved to be an adept administrator of her modest high school teacher's pension, which she used to pay her mortgage, keep up the house, and buy a car.

In 1979, Carlos Andrés Pérez, who'd lost popularity in his final years of government after being accused of corruption, passed the presidential sash to COPEI member Luis Herrera Campíns. Herrera's campaign slogan, "Where are the pennies?" was an attack on Pérez and his party, Democratic Action, who—even after years of abundance—left behind a country of fourteen million residents afflicted by poverty and broken promises.

The abundance of the Pérez years was now also viewed as a curse. Exorbitant oil incomes had bought the illusion of a strong economy. In practice, Venezuela was structurally impoverished, with economic sectors entirely dependent on the state's wasteful investment plan. Designed with the expectation that commodity revenues would increase, the plan hit a wall when prices rose only moderately in the second half of Pérez's term. His government resorted to incurring public debt to keep the petrodollars party going, compromising a weakened national economy.

Thus, a country with vast swathes of fertile land and large oil reserves imported most of what it consumed, while the state provided food and gasoline subsidies, generating a false idea of growth. This model, which in the Pérez years created a veneer of stability and wealth, was prolonged in the following years to cover up the social crisis as much as possible. Venezuela's economy was inextricably tied to crude, and when in the 1980s the sector reorganized in the wake of the decade's Arab-Israeli conflicts, the country suffered the effects of plummeting crude prices. With its vital dependence on imports, its foreign debt skyrocketed.

It was during this difficult transition to a challenging new decade that Mamá got pregnant again. Already overwhelmed by the high dose of steroids needed to control her arthritis pain, she tried to abort with some pills. But "the birth was meant to be," she told me when I was a child. I was born in 1981, in a public hospital, to an unemployed father and a retired mother. Papá was elated. "Your father went gaga as soon as he saw you," Mamá said. "He wanted a little girl." He took charge of feeding and bathing me in those first days. Pregnancy and childbirth had further weakened my mother's fragile, pain-racked body, preventing her from even picking me up.

They named me Paula, like my mother, but to avoid confusion, they called me Carola, which is how her family knows me to this day.

When Mamá started feeling better, Papá, by then over sixty, decided to open up another culinary enterprise. With no money to invest, he set up a modest coffee shop in front of the house, getting up at four each morning to make pastries and empanadas and prepare coffee and orange juice. Mamá was discouraged by how much Papá worked and how poorly he managed the business. "He doesn't know how to make the best of our blanket," she would say, doing the math on how each of his ventures ate up the small pool of cash she'd managed to save. I adored my father, and it upset me to hear Mamá talking like that. I was young and identified more with his dreamy spirit than with her pragmatism. It took me years to understand that her criticism was an expression of love.

His new venture failed in no time, and with an economic crisis around the corner, many other Venezuelans would also be forced to wake up from the dream.

Mamá was always saying we needed to "make the best of our blanket." But our blanket was long and wide compared to the hunger I would witness in the decades to come. We had free health care, and my mother was still collecting the pension that allowed her to pay her mortgage, even as inflation climbed into the double digits. The welfare state was our eternal benefactor. For Venezuelans, this was a given. The economic crisis of the 1980s was a rude awakening for a country that became poor just as quickly as its people had become rich in the 1970s.

President Herrera Campíns had run a campaign promising to solve our economic problems, but the abrupt devaluation of the bolívar against the US dollar and the end of the free exchange rate would be the thing that marked his administration. Oil prices started to fall in 1981, adding to the capital flight that had intensified in those years. The president declared the country insolvent to meet its international commitments. Arguing that he was protecting the international reserves, he interrupted the free trade of US dollars and instated exchange controls that codified three different rates on February 18, 1983—a day that came to be known as Viernes Negro. That stable exchange rate, which for decades had been less than 5 bolívares per dollar, was coming to an end. While the government maintained the value of 4.3 bolívares for public spending and debt payment, among other purposes, it created two other valuation tiers ranging from 6 to 10 bolívares per dollar. The sudden devaluation of the bolívar contributed to the collapse of a once-prosperous Venezuela. When people mentioned Viernes Negro to me as a child, they may as well have been crossing themselves—that's how deeply that day of mourning was burned into our national psyche.

The same expression echoed everywhere: "The party's over." Food price controls followed the exchange control. The country plunged into what felt like an unending catastrophe.

COPEI and Democratic Action blamed each other for the crisis, but the two parties continued to dominate elections and the political spectrum. In 1984, the social democrat Jaime Lusinchi sailed into the presidency with promises of a "great mandate."

In Caracas, which sits in a valley encircled by mountains and has a very different layout than Maracaibo, poverty was becoming much more visible. The city's hills filled with shanties as unemployment and the cost of living climbed.

Though we didn't have a lot of resources during those years, the house and Mamá's pension helped keep us afloat. Still, my parents had to make some difficult choices.

During the 1980s, public education wasn't what it had been two decades earlier: constant work stoppages and an undemanding curriculum meant you might not end up with a place at a public university. But it was an alternative, so my parents, unable to afford three private tuitions, enrolled my brothers in a public school. Mamá had other plans for me. She was convinced my one chance of getting into college was with a private education, and the only way to do this on a budget was by securing a coveted spot at a Catholic school, where the tuition was subsidized by the government. Though I didn't know it then, I wasn't Catholic. My father, an atheist, had refused to get us baptized. Plus I was too young to go to school. But these were mere details for Mamá, who lied about my faith, fudged my date of birth, and had me sit for the entrance exam. By the time the nuns discovered the truth, I'd been enrolled there for four years.

My mother would laugh when I asked about the methods she'd used to get me in. "When you're poor, you have to stay on your toes," she used to say, proud of her cunning. She believed in discipline and honesty, but she walked a fine line when it came to "criollo clever." She framed the minor subterfuges that we Venezuelans employed without considering ourselves corrupt—such as declaring more dependents to avoid taxes, or sweet-talking our way out of traffic violations—as necessary evils. At the end of the day, it was the politicians who were truly corrupt. How long were we, the poor, expected to keep handing money over to a government that stole from us, to a government that we blamed for the situation we were in? I didn't love how she made it happen, but I have to admit that without her initiative, my education would've been very different.

By the end of the 1980s, in the midst of an economic crisis driven by declining oil prices, my father had joined the growing ranks of the self-employed and reinvented himself as a school transportation driver. My mother's pension wasn't enough to cover tuition and books.

But my parents still managed to provide the basics. Though I didn't appreciate it at the time, every Sunday lunch featured either paella or squid in ink, pretty much the only Spanish customs Papá upheld. I only recognized our poverty, which my mother never failed to remind us about, when I went to my cousins' house.

My uncle Daniel was an engineer who owned a private business. My cousins had a Nintendo console and got to go to Disney World, a common tradition in 1970s Venezuela that had become a real privilege by the time we reached the '80s. My younger cousin had Barbies and collected autographs from Donald Duck and Mickey Mouse in a red notebook emblazoned with Mickey's famous silhouette. This was so far from my reality that I wasn't even jealous. I never thought it was possible for me to have what my younger cousin had.

My Catholic school was also a constant reminder of the position I occupied on the social ladder. All it took was one look at my off-brand uniform, and my classmates' official ones, to see our economic differences.

At Christmastime in steamy Maracaibo, people often decorated their houses with fake pines and artificial snow. My father, on the other hand, would track down a tree skeleton, paint it white, and stick it in a flowerpot. We'd decorate its branches with strings of apples, pears, and candy that we later ate during our holiday festivities. Even though I loved the tradition, I knew it was different, which is how I assimilated the idea that being poor meant being different. Everything at home was different, though not necessarily bad. It was as if we had the same things as the upper-middle class, just generic.

Ultimately, it was a matter of perspective. I understood that poverty has many layers, and that we didn't occupy a bottom one, regardless of what Mamá said.

In retrospect, her decision to send us siblings to different schools seems to have played a crucial role in defining the paths our lives would follow. Again, it was about perspective. Intellectually, I measured myself against my upper-middle-class peers, and my brothers did the same with their working-class peers. I was always looking up; they were looking down.

My mother justified this decision by saying that, for lack of money, she was forced to make strategic choices—that my brothers showed no interest in books, while I was always reading or writing plays for my stuffed animals. It didn't have to do with playing favorites, Mamá said; it had to do with merit. And there was also a safety issue. She couldn't bring herself to send her only daughter to a public school, where someone might hurt me. She felt confident that I was protected in a girls' school.

Papá did not hide who his favorite was. It was so obvious that even my mother's siblings gave him a hard time about it.

Thus an invisible wall was erected between my brothers and me. The three of us were very different, and it wasn't hard to see we were growing apart as we got older. They resented the special treatment I got from my father. Soon my mother started feeling uncomfortable, too. "You took my husband from me," she told me years later, her voice resigned.

I admired Papá so much that I copied everything he did. At night we "drank" together; he knocked back one Cuba libre after another, making me lemonade so I could keep up. He usually ate dinner later than the rest of the family, and I would wait for him. After our "drinks," we ate dinner together, just the two of us, and then sat in front of the house to stargaze. It was like he and I lived in a world my mother and brothers had no access to. In our private conversations, my father would talk about life in the concentration camp like it was the kind of thing that happened to everyone. In his stories, he was always a witness. The torture, the wounds, the humiliation, all happened to other people, not to him. He spoke of seeing a little boy die after a soldier crushed his skull, of seeing his fellow prisoners killed by soldiers who'd decided they were no longer useful. He told me about an officer who kept a framed piece of skin in his office and periodically refreshed it with blood. I don't know how Papá survived those four years. I also didn't understand that this wasn't normal. I thought all fathers went to war and woke up screaming every night. *Despite all the horrors, the war didn't break him,* I thought. My father was proud—so proud that even after the Spanish dictator Francisco Franco died in 1975, he never sought to recover his Spanish citizenship, which he'd lost during the war. And despite my mother's insistence on seeing Europe, my father believed that the place he had come from, which had caused him so much pain, was in his past, not his future. He was Venezuelan, end of discussion. For years I wondered if he really didn't want to go back, or if he was just afraid of being homesick again—for this home, his adopted one.

My relationship with Papá was so strong that the bulk of my child-hood memories consist of the time we spent together, our everyday routines. But according to my mother, he was turning me into a spoiled brat who lived in a different world from our family's reality, which was marked by poverty. This caused a lot of fights.

Because of our low budget and my mother's fixation on health, we had an unusual diet. We ate soya meat, sea salt (basically a salt rock in a bottle of water), raw cane sugar, and fresh eggs. Our house may have been small, but the surrounding property was large. My mother raised chickens on the open patio until the day one wall of the enclosure fell in, killing the black rooster that ruled the coop. So we ate the chickens, which my dad killed one by one over the large sink where we did our laundry. Then Mamá turned the patio into a small orchard with bananas, plantains, lemons, and watermelons. Our grocery list never included candy, cookies, or artificial drinks. At home, bottles of Coca-Cola were exclusively for my father's daily Cuba libres. There was almost no packaged food in the house, not even mayonnaise or tomato sauce. For a long time, Mamá wouldn't even buy traditional corn flour, choosing instead to grind corn every night.

My mother taught me several of her frugal home remedies: warm rings of white onion for the joints, red-onion juice for the flu, chamomile for inflammation, and, of course, the infallible aloe vera for anything and everything. She used to peel it and apply the clear pulp to all sorts of wounds, put it in a jar with a bit of water to make conditioner, mix it with lemon to treat sore throats, or take it alone as a digestive aid.

Her approach was handy in a country that seemed to be going deeper and deeper into crisis, with no end in sight. In Venezuela, where the agricultural sector had been squeezed out by oil, more than half the produce was imported. When oil income fell—thanks to price drops and OPEC's decision to decrease crude production—informal employment increased. By then most of my family members worked for themselves, selling food and other products from stores inside their houses. We lived in a country where taxes were rarely collected and dreams were the daily currency, so the cost of a business startup was basically setting up a shelf and putting things on it. Even my aunts, who'd worked as teachers, had retired, rounding out their state pensions with money from other undertakings.

Despite the crisis, my parents made sure we got to celebrate our birthdays with piñatas. That said, there was one piñata for all three of our birthdays. Mamá started cutting back on Christmas gifts as well. I would dream of a Barbie but get a rag doll instead. When I got upset, Mamá would tell me about all the times she and her siblings had to beg for toys. This is how she taught me about "the value of things." I couldn't picture Mamá begging for presents as a kid. It was hard to imagine her—so haughty and proud—begging for anything. "We have to make the best of our blanket," she'd say every time. And I didn't understand what she meant; I just wanted a Barbie.

Mamá put a lot of her effort into getting us food for the best price, while Papá dealt with any problems that cropped up at home, from painting the walls to waterproofing the roof. It had been a two-bedroom house, but my parents added a third bedroom when I was a kid. It was separated from theirs with just an unglazed window, which allowed both bedrooms to be cooled by the only air conditioner in the house.

My brothers slept in the bedroom on the second floor. They didn't have air-conditioning because we couldn't afford a second unit or the electric bills, but with two picture windows it was much cooler than the ground floor, where the Maracaibo heat made it almost impossible to sleep.

Papá had strung light bulbs all over the garage, where he loved to entertain Mamá's siblings almost every weekend. He would drag in a card table to serve rum that no one drank because it was always overshadowed by the whiskey my uncle brought. Conversations about politics were interspersed with family jokes. Talk of corruption and criticism of the political parties that had "ruined the country" and "stolen everything" was as common as seeing my aunt Elisa's husband drunk. Thanks to our strong rentier culture, people just couldn't wrap their heads around why we weren't swimming in money if we still had oil.

No one seemed happy with President Lusinchi and his promise of a "great mandate." His administration was coming to an end, and this man, who'd fought against the Pérez Jiménez dictatorship in the 1950s and been detained and tortured, roused an already-exhausted country.

Like in a telenovela, the last straw was the key role taken by his lover and private secretary, Blanca Ibáñez—nicknamed "la barragana," or "the paramour"—who was said to be the person actually governing the country, appointing ministers, making decisions about concessions, and approving military promotions. In Venezuela it wasn't uncommon for presidents to take lovers, but the power Ibáñez was rumored to wield was a sensitive topic, in part because of the corruption scandals that kept popping up all over the place. People thought of her as an upstart who'd taken the president down the wrong path, while Lusinchi was seen as a weak man who was being dominated.

As the 1980s came to a close, the country was roiling. All that remained from the golden days, when the middle class went on regular shopping trips to Miami, were anecdotes.

It was in that bleak landscape that Carlos Andrés Pérez, once a symbol of the country's wealth, decided to run for president again in 1988. Even though he was now sixty-six, he led an energetic campaign. A photo of him leaping over a puddle became the image of the moment. Venezuelans elected him handily, in what seemed like a last-ditch gamble of faith in politics—as though he really were a lucky charm, and bringing him back could restore an era of wealth. But as the country would quickly find out, things don't work that way.

Chapter 3

The Caracazo

In the late 1980s, the playwright José Ignacio Cabrujas claimed that "the notion of the state" in Venezuela "is all smoke and mirrors."[1] In one of his most famous interviews, Cabrujas said that "the advent of oil as an industry created something like a cosmogony in Venezuela. The state quickly took on a providential dimension. It shot from an era of slow development—slow like everything having to do with agriculture—to an era of miraculous, spectacular development."[2] During a time when Venezuelans were starting to feel disillusioned by their democracy, although it was often praised abroad, Cabrujas affirmed that any "candidate who does not promise paradise is suicidal. Why? Because the state has nothing to do with our reality. The state is a magnanimous wizard, a hope-laden titan in the pack of lies that is our government programs."[3]

---

1   Luis García Mora, Ramón Hernández, Trino Márquez, and Víctor Suárez, "El Estado del disimulo: La entrevista a Cabrujas," *Prodavinci*, October 21, 2020, https://prodavinci.com/el-estado-del-disimulo-la-entrevista-a-cabrujas-1/.
2   Mora et al., "El Estado del disimulo."
3   Mora et al., "El Estado del disimulo."

In his campaign, Pérez promised a return to the "Great Venezuela." For the nation, "Pérez was not the President. He was a wizard," Cabrujas wrote.[4] He was so popular that he made it possible for Democratic Action to remain in power after Lusinchi.

Papá had voted for Pérez not for the country's lost wealth but because he thought Pérez represented the people and the public welfare system. My father was a man of the Left, and even though Pérez had stepped down from government almost a decade earlier in a cloud of suspected corruption, Papá still admired him. To my father, Pérez's relevance in Venezuelan history was undeniable. He had fought for the country's democracy decades earlier, and in Papá's romantic heart, this was an unbreakable bond. My mother voted for Pérez to satisfy my father, but as far as she was concerned, all politicians were "cut from the same cloth."

Pérez's first significant measure was a package of economic adjustments that contrasted sharply with his presidential inauguration, which was so luxurious it was dubbed a "coronation."

As people awaited their return to wealth, the president announced "El Gran Viraje," or "the Great Turn." Also known as "El Paquetazo," it was Pérez's proposal to leave behind the safety net of the past decades' populist development model and embrace a competitive global market supported by the International Monetary Fund, a change nobody was prepared for. During his first month in power, saddled with enormous debt and few resources, Pérez announced a gradual increase in the cost of public transit, the liberalization of interest rates and price control, and a reduction in the fiscal deficit, among other measures. All of this triggered stockpiling, which sent certain foods flying off the shelves.

But what proved most unpopular and catalyzed national frustration was the government's decision to increase the price of gas—an enormous miscalculation. Just as Venezuelans take for granted that the sea

---

4   Mora et al., "El Estado del disimulo."

off the coast is turquoise and warm, they assumed that if there was oil to spare, then gas should be cheap, if not free.

The response to the price hike was a social explosion.

On February 27, 1989, drivers at a bus terminal on the outskirts of Caracas decided to raise ticket prices before the fuel price increase went into effect. Passengers protested, and within minutes their outrage had spread like wildfire. The capital was engulfed in chaos that did not reflect our traditional Caribbean cheer. "The hills came down," people said, alluding to the geography of Caracas, where the middle and upper classes lived in the valley and the poor and the working class in the growing slums on the slopes bordering the city.

The news was filled with images of people looting supermarkets, police overwhelmed by the rage in the streets, disoriented soldiers shooting in every direction, and bodies sprawled on the ground. Within forty-eight hours, the situation in Caracas had become so dire that the minister of interior and justice, Alejandro Izaguirre, choked up and left the podium before finishing a televised message meant to assure viewers that everything was under control. Though the state managed to rein in the pandemonium over the next three days with the use of outsize force, the protest was a clear sign of dissatisfaction, one that took Pérez by surprise. Christened the "Caracazo," the popular uprising left hundreds dead. Though there was no unrest in Maracaibo, we watched the news slack jawed. The Caracazo marked the beginning of a new era. From then on, the country would take another turn, uprooting what was ostensibly the most stable democracy in Latin America. It was our before-and-after moment.

Dissatisfaction with the new government—which had promised riches but was now recording inflation rates topping 80 percent—took root across the entire country.

My cousins stopped traveling to Disney World, and my uncle shuttered his small pool-cleaning business when he ran out of clients. Like my father, Tía Elisa became a school transportation driver; her husband, who ran a shop that sold and repaired air-conditioner units and refrigerators, was making less and less money. Family parties became sparer and less frequent.

Even though I was a child, I could tell that the crisis the adults were always talking about was the reason for my mom's "paquetazo" at home. She stopped buying new uniforms for me, and I started reusing my older cousins' books. But I kept going to my school, we had food on the table, and my brothers and I were still allowed small luxuries like ice cream and sweets on Sundays. It became a recurring theme for Mamá to say that Papá had squandered too many opportunities. "When he came to Venezuela, they were selling land for pennies and he didn't buy any," she used to repeat, a futile exercise in mourning what could have been.

I didn't understand how my father could be so detached from money and material things yet so obsessed with not wasting a single speck of food. He would tell us about the war and how you could lose everything in one day, but I didn't understand—how could someone really lose everything? I was never able to feel his fear. Despite my parents' impoverished pasts, I took everything I had for granted. In any case, I never left food on my plate because my father's rule was that whoever didn't finish their lunch would have the leftovers for dinner. "One day, when you don't have enough to eat, you'll remember this," he said. The issue for me wasn't hunger, but how much I hated eating cold leftovers.

Obsessed as he was with wastefulness, he once reprimanded me for letting a dab of toothpaste fall in the sink. He made me scrape it up and put it back on my toothbrush. "During the war, we had nothing," he said with the sad eyes I could never bear to meet. I still think of this incident every time I brush my teeth. If a smidge of toothpaste falls onto the porcelain, I scrape it up right away. Despite our age difference, and although my country had nothing to do with his suffering, I was raised as a postwar child.

My father, who listened to joropo and drank rum while cooking, also loved showing me the atlas because he thought it was fundamental that I learn the world's capitals as a child. He spoke passionately about the Cold War and was shocked as he watched the fall of the Berlin Wall on our TV. Thanks to him I had a politicized childhood. He talked to me about Pinochet, Trujillo, Videla, Viola, and Galtieri. When I was ten years old, he made me watch *Night of the Pencils*, an Argentinian film that follows the arrest of seven young men and women who took part in the 1976 student strike. It was far from being a children's film. I guess he wanted to expose me to his ideals. He also spoke to me about Cuba and utopia. He'd always had a nationalist, anti-US stance; he considered that country an invader and a threat to Latin America. Papá didn't just believe in a better world; he'd fought for one, which I took to mean that he stood by his convictions. He taught me to love the country and the continent that he adopted, or that adopted him. I have vague memories of my mother trying to convince him to "return" to Europe—she dreamed about living in Paris and seeing the Eiffel Tower—but I don't remember any decisive moves on his part.

Some Venezuelans did migrate during this time of social and economic crisis, among them two of my older cousins who lived in San Cristóbal and decided to move to the United States, where one of their wives had family.

Around that time, there was an uptick in violence, and we felt it on our skin, as our house was under threat.

At home there was a fence separating the sidewalk from our garage, where Mamá parked her car. It was a regular fence, easy to jump over, but until then we never thought of that as a problem. Both the front and back doors of our house were made of wood, with glass windows and basic locks. One night, Andrés, who always stayed up in the living room late into the night, heard a noise and saw shadows moving behind the kitchen window. We were all awakened by his screaming. Papá threatened to shoot, which was a bluff since we didn't have any firearms, and the burglars ran off. The following day, Mamá hired a blacksmith to install iron bars on both doors. That evening, there was another attempted break-in. Mamá decided to have bars installed in every window. Before long all the houses we saw had barred windows. Break-ins were becoming an everyday occurrence.

With the death toll from the Caracazo, which in turn fueled further violence in the country, the murder rate shot up to more than ten deaths per one hundred thousand people. It would only go up from there.

As the quality of life deteriorated, students and workers staged an increasing number of protests. The sentiment nationwide was that the people had been betrayed by the political class. In Venezuela, home of nineteenth-century liberator Simón Bolívar, the longing for a savior never dies. Bolívar was Venezuela's all-time hero, a cult figure whose name we learned in elementary school and was hammered into us in high school, where there was a class devoted exclusively to him. He is revered in several Latin American countries for leading the wars of independence against the Spanish conquistadors. The courage of the general who crossed the Andean Cordillera on horseback and the oratory of the man who mobilized the masses with his speeches are part of Venezuela's legacy.

It makes sense, then, that our political leaders had been using his speeches for decades, appealing to patriotic sentiment and social justice. And in the midst of the greatest economic crisis in our country's contemporary history, a man appeared out of nowhere, having mastered like no other this age-old strategy for connecting emotionally with Venezuelans.

The day Hugo Chávez came into our lives, on February 4, 1992, started the same as any other. I was ten and getting ready for school when I heard the gate open. I didn't have time to wonder why—my father marched in and immediately turned on the 14-inch TV. That's when we realized it wasn't just another day.

Dissatisfied soldiers had launched a coup during the night. Sitting next to my brothers, also half-dressed in their school uniforms, I watched a tank try to break through the front gates of the Palacio de Miraflores in Caracas as President Carlos Andrés Pérez assured everyone that the situation was under control. Reporters phoned in from Valencia, Maracay, and Maracaibo, our Maracaibo, where "the rebels" had stormed the governor's residence just a few blocks from our house. The street remained silent, like a Sunday during a holiday, and we watched TV for hours until the televised surrender of the then-unknown lieutenant colonel Hugo Chávez.

Young and tall, in an olive uniform and red beret that would go on to become his trademark, "El Comandante Chávez" appeared before the cameras on that chaotic Tuesday morning with a subversive message of surrender that struck a chord. The government had the coup under control, but Chávez's short speech would be studied for years: it wasn't every day you saw a soldier and Academia Militar graduate who'd just been detained for inciting revolt give a serene, composed warning that "new possibilities will arise again." The military officer opened his speech with "For now the objectives we set ourselves have not been achieved in the capital city," and this "For now"—and its implication that this was a beginning, not an end—resonated with the people.

As he watched the drama play out on TV, my father's demeanor changed. He, who'd rebuilt his life in a democratic Venezuela, seemed saddened. He had plenty of reasons to fear military action and a coup. But he could also empathize with young soldiers who risked their lives for an ideal. Years later, I could see how that day brought him contradictory feelings. Even as he was rooting for democracy, he was seduced by the savoir faire of this man Chávez—who, before going to prison for leading a failed coup, vowed "to take the country toward a better destiny." It was the first time I remember my parents kind of agreeing on politics. Mamá was intrigued by Chávez too, but her process was more straightforward: she was fed up with the political party system, with elections, and with AD and COPEI.

I skipped classes that day, which in fact made it a bit of a holiday. I didn't understand exactly what was going on, but I had the sense that we were living in unsettling times, that there was always something happening on the news. I could feel my parents' agitation, but I have no memories of my older brother Luis looking affected. Being the kind of person who didn't get emotional about things that had no immediate, tangible impact on his life, he was indifferent. But Andrés, my second-oldest brother, was more engaged. He seemed excited—to the point of going to the street and timidly writing "Long live Chávez" on a neighboring wall with a tub of my black paint.

My parents kept watching the news, each with one eye on the small TV screen and the other on the kitchen or the kids. In Caracas, where political leaders were quick to condemn the coup, one congressional voice stood out. Rafael Caldera, who had served as president from 1969 to 1974 and was an opponent of Pérez, asserted that the country was in a "serious situation" and called on the government to "immediately address the profound rectifications the country is calling for." He foretold the political vulnerability of hungry, cynical people:

> *It is difficult to ask the people to sacrifice themselves for freedom and democracy when they think that freedom and democracy are incapable of giving them food to eat, of preventing the astronomical rise in the cost of subsistence, or of placing a definitive end to the terrible scourge of corruption that, in the eyes of the entire world, is eating away at the institutions of Venezuela with each passing day.*[5]

---

5 "Caldera: Dos discursos (1989/1992)," https://rafaelcaldera.com/caldera-dos-discursos-19891992/, trans. Steven Levitsky and Daniel Ziblatt, *How Democracies Die* (New York: Crown, 2018), 17.

Caldera's speech, which was considered opportunistic and electioneering, put him on the map for the next presidential election. But Venezuelans still had a great deal more to go through before going to the ballots.

Many saw Chávez and the other officers who led the February coup as patriots. They'd stood up to a corrupt government, and had done so in the name of justice. Chávez, whose origins were humble and whose skin was dark, was viewed as a man of the people, a sort of national hero.

Although the streets were calm, the country was emotionally tense, and this feeling even seeped into one of the country's main cultural mediums: the telenovela. In June, the oldest television network in Venezuela premiered *Por estas calles*, a show about life in the barrios, violence, inequality, and the economic crisis. Mamá didn't watch telenovelas and didn't let us watch them either, but she made an exception for us in this case, because it was about life in Venezuela. I was eleven years old and excited to watch my first telenovela. The show made an impact on me. Night after night the country followed a fictional story that depicted its reality. Suddenly, there was no more escape valve.

Pérez had barely recovered from the coup when on November 27, 1992, several high-ranking officials launched another coup. This one was less popular and more cruel. Fighter jets flew over Caracas as we watched on our little knobbed television. Although the coups were not backed by the majority of the military, they exposed the facts that the armed forces were fractured and people had lost faith in democracy as a form of government. It wasn't that they wanted to live under a dictatorship, but they blamed the political parties for the corruption, insecurity, and high cost of living. It was becoming clear to me that coups were going to be an everyday thing—for a while, on days when I hadn't finished my homework, I believed a military uprising could save me from going to class, the way a sudden fever might.

So, the president had lost the support of the people and the military, as well as his own party. Relations between president and party had been tense since before his electoral campaign. Gradually, the idea gained ground that the only way out of the mess was for him to leave. In May 1993, the president who'd promised to lead us out of the pit was removed from office, accused of embezzlement and misappropriating funds.

I have few memories of those months. But I do remember that it was a sad, difficult time. I was terrified someone would break into our house; crime was the only thing people talked about in the neighborhood. For a while, my parents, my siblings, and I took turns at night staying awake so we could warn the others if we heard any noise.

Political instability frightened my parents, and economic instability suffocated them. Mamá cut her expenses down to the bare necessities. With her salary whittled away by inflation, Papá decided to use his car as a por puesto in the afternoons. On weekends he bought bananas from a popular fruit market and resold them for a small profit outside the house. One morning, as I watched him unload the bananas, I started crying. At seventy-three years old, my father had no choice but to work harder and harder every day.

Mamá's health was also declining.

Her precarious physical condition had affected my relationship with her when I was a child. I don't have any memories of us playing together, and even though there are photos of me sitting in her lap, one of my frustrations is not remembering many hugs. Her arthritis was so debilitating that whenever I tried to go near her, she'd yell at me not to touch her, terrified of the pain. Mamá was thin and wore partial dentures to compensate for the teeth she'd lost as a child in pre-boom Venezuela, when going to the dentist was a luxury only the rich could afford. She had surgical scars on her abdomen and would accumulate a few more on her hips and knees. And yet there weren't any grays peppering her black hair, nor wrinkles webbing her round face, the result of years of cortisone injections.

She had good days. But on bad ones, when the pain hit, she couldn't even comb her hair. One day, in a fit of rage, she broke every single one of the china pieces on her dressing table. Another time, she practically crashed the car on her way home from my school. She didn't know how to deal with the pain or with the restrictions her illness imposed on her life.

Mamá took pain medication daily and would need to for the rest of her life. As the years passed, she came to depend on other treatments: calcium, vitamins, and hormones. There was an infinite array of pill bottles at home. Little by little, the house began to resemble a hospital. She also had equipment for muscle therapy, breathing exercises, and massages. Social security covered some of these treatments, but in a country gripped by political turmoil, hospitals were not immune to the economic crisis, and medical resources were starting to dwindle.

I grew up using the public health system. I remember the ER entrance at the public hospital that was a five-minute drive from home. It was an old building, like a colonial house with a big courtyard, painted in blue and white. We went there often for emergencies, not only because of Mamá's condition but because we were kids. Between broken bones and late-night fevers, we visited that place at least once a week. Sometimes we might have to wait ten or twenty minutes to be seen by a doctor, but everything was free, including the medicines we took home. That was another privilege I took for granted back then. My parents wouldn't have been able to afford medical bills or health insurance in those days. For nonemergency appointments, we went to the Ministry of Education's free health center, a benefit of my mother's retirement package as a public school teacher. She was obsessed with health and took us for biannual blood tests and dentist consultations, no matter what. I went with her so often to the health center that the nurses and doctors there essentially watched me grow up. Mamá's medical history spanned two encyclopedic volumes—and that didn't include her emergency visits to the public hospital. To this day, I can still remember her patient file number: 1027.

When I was a kid, I thought Mamá could die at any moment because that's what she was always telling us. I was well acquainted with hospitals and ambulances, having called them since I was five. At some point during those years, my brothers and I got used to the noise of sirens outside our home: when we weren't calling the police because someone was trying to break in, we were calling an ambulance because Mom wasn't feeling well. The arthritis affected her legs the most—legs she adored because she loved to dance. According to my aunt, Mamá was very good at it. So good that I stopped dancing in front of her at parties to avoid her criticism. One time she looked at me and said, "You don't look like my daughter. You're your father's daughter," implying that I had him to thank for my nonexistent dancing skills.

When she blew out her birthday candles or ate grapes on New Year's Eve, Mamá always wished for the same thing: good health. One of her favorite refrains was "Health is everything," and she would cry— dry-eyed because of her illness—when she talked about the hereditary autoimmune disease that consumed her body and terrified me because I could see the havoc it wreaked. This, she predicted, would be my fate too. She was obsessed with taking care of me—and preparing me. She used to say that no one had warned her about the disease. "Because you had me, you'll know what to do when the pain starts," she often said. So she ran regular blood tests on me and got my teeth checked often. Everything for free. But then the crisis started to impact the health system as well, a change we were quick to notice. It became harder to find an ambulance. The emergency room was busier and lacked some of their usual resources. Patients had to bring medical materials like needles or bandages to the public ERs, which started working at reduced capacity at night. Stories about patients who died going from one hospital to another, trying to find medical care, were becoming more common. That's why the night my father, who almost never went to the doctor, asked to be taken to the hospital for extreme pain, Mamá drove him straight to a private clinic.

My father was so fascinating to me that I didn't realize he was old and sick. I had no idea that Papá—who smoked, drank rum religiously, and never missed a chance to eat fried food—had a weak heart and water in his lungs. He had chest pain, but I wasn't aware that chest pain was a symptom of heart failure. I didn't even know what heart failure was. My mother obviously did, which is why, even though our blanket didn't stretch that far, entrusting him to a public hospital was a risk she wasn't willing to take.

My father was admitted to the emergency room without advance payment. It was a different time in Venezuela, when nurses and doctors did not delay medical care for a cardiac patient because of administrative issues. It was the middle of the night, the family could pay in the morning. But we didn't have the money. I don't know what went through Mamá's head at that moment. She always had a habit of believing things would work out. Sometimes I feel I've inherited this quality from her. Or maybe it's just a manifestation of our Caribbean way of living, like being alive is simply an act of faith. The fact is that for years I watched as things kept on working out for her, one way or another.

Early the next morning, my mother took me to visit Papá. It was November 1993. I was twelve years old, and it was only my second time in a private hospital. She left me next to his hospital bed while she went to check on my brothers at home. He was pallid and frail, like he'd been stripped of all his superpowers. I watched as he coughed blood into a handkerchief, too weak to get up and go to the bathroom. He complained about the fact that Mamá had dropped me off at the hospital without breakfast and told me to go home. An aunt took me back to the house. When I saw my brother, I burst into tears. "Papá is going to die," I sobbed. Luis gave me breakfast and said he'd take me back to the hospital, but he didn't want to hear me "blubbering"—a classic example of my mother's style of "affection." I walked beside him, choking back tears. My father was admitted to intensive care and died a couple of hours later. The only thing he left us were our memories of him, a life story we didn't fully understand, and an old pickup truck that spent more time in the shop than it did on the streets. He died without a penny to his name; any money he made had always gone straight into our home. My mom called his family in Caracas, and his three children from his first marriage came immediately. They were decades older than me—the eldest was practically the same age as my mother. Given that they were more financially stable, they took care of his medical bill with a couple of plastic cards—something I'd seen only in movies. I remember Mamá packing up without crying, and saying to me, "Things are going to be different around here. You need to grow up." I thought she didn't love him and that she didn't love me, either. She was so harsh, always talking about crises and savings, while my dad was always hugging me and telling me how much I meant to him. I tried to grow up, but I didn't know what that meant. That's about the time I became introspective and started to write.

"I missed your father all the time, but only cried about it when you were in school," Mamá told me years later. She didn't have it easy. She was a widow, a pensioner, ill. It was sheer determination that helped her keep the house and bring up three kids on her own, in a country that was falling to pieces. Her hopes of strolling along the banks of the Seine or seeing the Eiffel Tower were gone forever.

Chapter 4

Beauty and the Beast

The 1990s started as a hopeless decade for Venezuela. People were sick of corruption scandals, which they saw as the main cause of the country's misfortunes. Former president Caldera, who had given that ambiguous speech in Congress after the February 4 coup, capitalized on the wave of discontent to try to find his way back into office.

To convince the population that he was the face of the new politics, he disassociated himself from COPEI, one of the two parties that had governed the country for decades. The trick was good enough to help him win the election in 1993, at age seventy-seven, but it didn't move people like my mom, who felt he was more of the same. She didn't vote, and she wasn't the only one; that election registered a record abstention rate of nearly 40 percent, more than double the previous record.

In addition to the political instability, the economic problems, and the uptick in violence, weeks before Caldera assumed the presidency at the beginning of 1994, an unprecedented banking crisis caused by financial speculation left millions of people terrified of losing what little money they had.

To rescue part of the private banking system, the Caldera administration spent more than half that year's national budget. But the bankers fled with part of the money, leaving Venezuela submerged in one of the worst banking crises in the region.

Everyone had lost faith in the parties, and now they were losing faith in the banks and the elites.

Against that somber backdrop, the only people who weren't demoralized were in the military. Locked away in their barracks for nearly two years, the soldiers who'd stormed the streets during the attempted coups were now regarded as saviors.

It was not surprising then that Caldera had promised in his campaign to release them. And so Chávez, among others, was acquitted in March 1994.

In his first interview upon his release from prison, the retired lieutenant colonel announced that he would work to build a national movement that would restore power to the people. The oratorial prowess he had shown in the brief speech that made him famous in 1992 was once again evident. He immediately began touring the country, armed with the red beret that would become his signature and with his vision of cleaning up the partisan spectrum—a new politics.

Meanwhile, violence took over our day-to-day, so much so that our vocabulary was contaminated by aggression, even when we were trying to be romantic. A common pickup line at the time went something like "I'd love to kidnap you." Although Mamá didn't have the money lying around, she decided to fortify our house even more, using concrete to reinforce the parts she considered most vulnerable. There were times when she didn't sleep, out of fear that someone would break into the house or poison our dog, Laica, who was too big to sleep inside with us.

My oldest brother, Luis, had just graduated from high school in 1993 and started working in a clothing store. Meanwhile, Mamá kept me in private school with help from an uncle and my best friend's mother. Worried that putting me in public school would ruin my chances of getting into the university, she'd swallowed her pride and accepted the money.

It was the most difficult time we'd ever experienced as a family. Electricity was so expensive that for several years, Mamá metered our utility consumption. She handled her pension with wartime frugality; still, currency devaluation and increasing inflation slowly ate away at it until there was almost nothing left. Our blanket had shrunk, but we had food and a roof over our heads. Mamá managed to finish paying off the house because thanks to state subsidies, her mortgage was utterly immune to inflation. The terms were so ridiculously favorable that toward the end of the loan, she just fished around the house for sofa change to make the payments.

In 1995, Venezuela was in recession. For the past two years, inflation had been the highest in the region, and now it was about to cross over into the triple digits. People could barely cover a basic food basket with their salaries, and most of the population lived in either poverty or extreme poverty. "The middle class doesn't exist anymore," my aunts and uncles would complain at the occasional weekend family gathering. They would also share anecdotes about my father, smiling at their memories of him "and his war stories—Jesús was always talking about war." The fact was that Papá's tales of hunger and destitution sounded like they were from another planet, even for those of us living in conditions of increased austerity.

While Chávez traveled around the country urging people not to vote in the upcoming election as a protest against Venezuela's partisan system, one of his co-conspirators from the February 1992 coup was running for regional office in my home state. Francisco Arias Cárdenas, who'd led the coup in Zulia, now hoped to take the reins by getting elected. Convinced that only the military could make real change at that point, Mamá did more than vote for him. At the age of fifty, with advanced arthritis, she protested in the street when the electoral authority announced that Arias Cárdenas had lost to a candidate from the Democratic Action party. The pressure from the streets was so high that a recount was called and Arias Cárdenas was declared governor of the second most important state in the country.

Even though Democratic Action and COPEI still dominated the political landscape, the precedent established by Arias Cárdenas made it clear that things were changing and that political outsiders could capitalize on national discontent. Venezuelans had not given up on finding a savior. This is how in 1997, when two elite politicians approached Chávez to discuss his chances of winning an election—people were summoning his name as an alternative for president in open-response surveys—Chávez set aside his abstentionist policies and founded the Fifth Republic Movement (MVR), the political party under which he would run for president the following year, promising to re-found the republic.

At the time, Mamá was in decent health. To pad her income, she fixed up the front of the house for a small business venture that was popular in that time of crisis: a lottery retailer. Just as Venezuelans are forever awaiting a miracle in politics, they also believe in magical solutions for their financial hurdles. People with money worked as de facto bankers, opening stands where three winning numbers were awarded per draw. The bankers kept almost all the proceeds, though they were responsible for paying the awards and funding the points of sale. For people like my mother who owned a location to set up a lottery stand, the gains were small but dependable. She didn't have to pay rent, taxes, or wages, given that she and I were the only ones working there.

Around this time, Luis fell in love with a girl and moved to San Cristóbal, where my mother had lived as a child. By now my brothers and I were more distant than we'd been during our childhood. My mother, who loved to play the blame game, chalked it up to the fact that my father picked favorites. In hindsight, it's possible this was part of the problem. Every family has its share of resentment and trauma, of little moments that can permanently weaken a relationship. Hard as I tried, I couldn't pinpoint any singular turning points that caused us to drift apart. But they seemed clear to my brothers—especially Andrés, the middle child, the filling in the sibling sandwich. He was always the unruliest and Mamá's main cause for concern. We went long periods without talking. He held a grudge not only against our mother, but also against Luis and me. According to his version of events, which was founded on bitterness and resentment, our parents had given us more financial and emotional support than they had him. He had a temper, which wasn't uncommon in our family, but he was also the kind of person who was always finding someone else to blame for his failures, convinced the universe was out to get him.

In his good moods, Andrés could make me laugh nonstop. I saw myself in him physically—we had similar facial expressions and the same smile. I wanted him to love me. I wanted him to realize I didn't hate him, but it became harder and harder to get through to him. He held parallel versions of events in his head. He used to say that he was raised on his own, that Mamá didn't feed him when he was a kid, or neglected him in different ways. I couldn't figure out if he was just being cynical or if he really believed the things he said. Either way, he always resented Mamá for leaving him in a care home when he was a toddler.

Andrés was quite the character. When he was a kid, he was always reenacting war scenes with green plastic soldiers on the living room floor. People used to say he was "a piece of work" because he couldn't go a week without trying to set fire to something. Papá, my eternal prince charming, had been his ogre, trying to discipline him the only way he knew how—with the belt. That didn't help, and it may have even made matters worse. As the years went by, Andrés amassed kilos and kilos of rage. My father hit Andrés with the belt more than any of us, and eventually this felt normal. You're born into a particular house and everything around you seems normal, it becomes the definition of "normal"—until you start comparing it with what you see in other houses. Those were different times, and Andrés wasn't an easy kid. He could be aggressive to a point that made us scared. He would beat Luis and me, especially me, the one he resented most. My mother didn't approve of him hitting us, but she also did not approve of the way Papá treated him. At one point she tried hiring a therapist, but it didn't work out.

Andrés wanted to be a pilot but never met the requirements. After finishing high school in 1994, he didn't know what to do. Though it wasn't easy to get a spot at a public university, my mother, resigned to the fact that Luis was no scholar, insisted on helping Andrés get into the University of Zulia, her alma mater. She succeeded. But instead of studying, my brother threw himself into student politics. While Andrés had been difficult to get on track, he seemed to have found a passion in a youth movement that was constantly causing stoppages across public universities. Mamá fretted. More than once, she found herself at the School of Humanities asking for news of her son, who would sometimes disappear for days during a protest. My mother expressed her concern with anger. Instead of saying she wanted to know where her son was, she would complain about how irresponsible he was, "playing with rocks" in the streets instead of going to class.

Andrés was known as "el peluca" for his long hair. Almost no one knew his real name, though this changed in 1997, when I entered the university and people realized we were siblings. I was impressed when I saw his nickname painted onto a bridge that stretched across a wide avenue, connecting the university to the student cafeteria. Word in the halls was that he was one hell of a leader. One day, as I carpooled to the university, we were stopped by a group of students in the movement who'd blockaded the avenue and set fire to a truck—as they often did when protesting one of the hundreds of things that had gone wrong during that grueling decade. One of them came up to the window. His hair was loose, and a black bandanna concealed most of his face. I assumed he would tell us to get out, but when he saw me sitting in the front seat, he left without a word. As the driver thanked his lucky stars, I watched the man with the sad eyes dodge cars while directing the crowd of fired-up students and wondered if Papá would have been proud to see his son fighting for a cause he believed in, or if he would have simply reprimanded him.

"All this nonsense is for deadbeats. Universities are for studying, end of story," my mother said that night, annoyed, when I told her I'd seen Andrés at the protests that had kept me from class.

Every so often, my brother's nickname showed up in the papers. One time, we even spotted him in a photograph—slender, waving a flag on the roof of a bus at a protest in Caracas. But Andrés gave up on changing the world when he realized he didn't have a gift for political negotiations and could wind up behind bars at any moment. He dropped out of the university and joined the police academy without telling us. It wasn't hard for him to keep this a secret. He'd left home a few months earlier, when Mamá threw him out of the house during one of our countless arguments, which could go from verbal to physical in a matter of seconds. But that was just the straw that broke the camel's back. Even though Mamá loved him, and surely he loved her, it was like there were two different people inside him: the violent man with zero empathy who tried to squeeze the utility out of everything and the suffering man who felt despised by those around him. Neither of them was easy to live with.

Even though Andrés felt he was the sole object of Mamá's antipathy, she was no different with the rest of us. Luis came back home to live, but Mamá forced him to move in with his girlfriend when she found out the woman was pregnant, to "take responsibility for his actions."

By early 1998, Mamá and I were living at home alone. We regularly heard footsteps on the roof, or saw people jumping over the neighbors' fence through the window. Unlike Mamá, I was scared to death. "Don't worry," she would tell me as she picked up the phone to call the cops. Even though the country was in chaos, she was relatively healthy and her pension covered us both.

Though I'd sworn to go to law school, I gave up at the last minute, following the advice of a professor who didn't think I had what it took to navigate the judicial system. I didn't know what else to do, so I chose a career where I got to write, which I'd enjoyed doing since I was a kid.

Mamá was disappointed by my decision to study journalism, but I knew she was glad I enjoyed school and didn't "waste time" like my brothers.

I started journalism school in 1998, just as Chávez was running for president. Even though he was popular, the country seemed to favor his opponent: Irene Sáez, a former beauty queen whose first foray into politics was as mayor of Chacao, a municipality in the Caracas metropolitan area whose residents were predominantly middle and upper class.

Beautiful as a Barbie, with a leonine mane of golden hair, Sáez represented what the majority of Venezuelan women dreamed of becoming: a queen. After oil and baseball, the pageant was our most robust institution. Every year, the Miss Venezuela contest crowned a winner to represent the country in the Miss Universe pageant, as well as a runner-up to compete for the title of Miss World. In 1981, the year I was born, two blondes made history. Irene Sáez, our queen, sat on the Miss Universe throne, while Pilín León, a perfect 90-60-90—the ratio that epitomized Venezuelan beauty—was crowned Miss World.

Like the rest of the country, Mamá was a fan of the Miss Venezuela competition. While Papá made me reel off the names of capitals, cities, presidents, and important dates, she taught me the beauty primer: which Misses had won each contest and in which year. Practically everyone tried to usher their daughters onto that path, even my mom. When I was six or seven years old, I was convinced my legs were beauty-pageant material. I knew nothing about aesthetics, but my mother—goodness knows why—was always saying I had shapely legs. "The pediatrician agrees. She may well end up as Miss Venezuela," my mother used to brag, blinded by her blue-sky optimism. I never dared to try, but my mom kept watching the contest every year, where incredible beauties like Sáez showed their bodies in swimsuits and sparkling dresses.

One of the most cited clichés in the 1998 presidential campaign coverage was to refer to the opponents as "the beauty and the beast." It was as if some Venezuelans could not look themselves in the mirror. Chávez was much closer to being the face of the country. But his imminent triumph was only acknowledged in the final stretch of the campaign.

Although my mom admired Sáez, her heart was with Chávez. I tried to convince her not to vote for him. I didn't like military men. I'd learned to associate them with the bloody Latin American dictatorships from the 1970s that my dad taught me about. But she went out to vote with newfound fervor. Someone had made her believe things could be different. She asked me to go with her to the polling place to help her read the ballot; she didn't wear glasses and had minor vision problems. But when we got there, she decided she didn't trust me, and asked a young soldier to help her instead. That became another one of our arguments as our politics continued to diverge.

My mother and I always had a complicated relationship. Very rarely did we voice any mutual admiration. She liked to say that of her three children, I was the one who had driven her craziest as a teen. "Just like your father," she would say when she wanted to deal the final blow in an argument. Being like my father was equivalent to living impulsively, head permanently in the clouds.

Mamá was strict, and even though I was headstrong, she was able to keep me on a tight leash until I finished university; even there I had a curfew. I wasn't much different from any college student in their twenties, but in her eyes I was motivated purely by rebellion against her. She got this notion because, even though I respected and admired her, I never told her that and instead picked silly arguments with her.

The problem was that I was still grieving my dad—and somehow blaming her for all the times Andrés hit me, for how cold she was with me, for being sick most of my life, and for making me feel that I needed to be strong, that I couldn't disappoint her. She was so strong, she barely ever cried. Meanwhile, I had to choke back tears every time I thought about Papá or about how lonely I felt despite being raised with two brothers.

I missed Papá so much that I think I tried to be more like him, or what I remembered of him. Mamá didn't like that I smoked and drank and went to parties. She thought my college friends were "bad influences." I was young and arrogant and thought I was nothing like her. I didn't show interest in having a house, a husband, children. I learned to juggle and wanted to run away with the circus—that might have been my only true rebellion. But I wanted to finish college first. Dropping out was unthinkable; I couldn't do that to her. My parallel life outside the university, where I juggled on street corners, embarrassed her.

I loved Mamá and I wanted to reassure her that everything was fine, that things were under control, but every time she scolded me for something, I would sing the Vallenato song by Carlos Vives where a womanizing husband asks his wife to let him enjoy partying freely. I would croon, laughing as Mamá rolled her eyes and turned away from me. Even though I laughed, I felt increasingly misunderstood, and I pulled away from her.

I'll admit I was impressed by her political fervor for Chávez. I understood that she was attracted to his background in the armed forces. Clearly, she thought we needed a new version of Pérez Jiménez to get the house in order.

But she was also full of contradictions. Looking back, I think she was just a product of her time. If the price of oil hadn't plummeted in the 1980s and poverty hadn't skyrocketed, if the people hadn't revolted and a military man hadn't entered the scene like a new messiah, my mother would've continued to live off the state and not given any of it much thought. Instead, she made as much sense as she could of the circumstances according to her belief system. Class resentment had been germinating inside her for years, and even though she wanted to identify with the elite, she knew they existed in a world where she would be not just out of place but actively disdained. This is one reason she embraced Chávez, despite not wanting to be lumped into the same category as the working poor, the people living in the barrios, with whom she did not identify. Back then, when she was on intimate terms with "Chavismo," she had spouted the revolutionary narrative that traditional politicians were the masters of the valley, as the Caracas elite came to be popularly called, and had ruined the country with their ambition, neglecting the working poor and pushing them into the barrios—until El Comandante arrived, vowing to bring dignity to the people and build the country we'd never been able to have.

Anti-politics had been the trend since Pérez's second term. But people like my mom believed that Chávez was different. He promised to end corruption and instability and improve quality of life for the poor, who had been forgotten by decades of calcified bipartisan power disconnected from the people. Chávez had rekindled hope in most of the country, and he was going to relaunch the republic.

Chapter 5

You Won't Be Back

On December 6, 1998, Chávez made history. At the age of forty-four, the man who had barged into our lives during a failed coup became the first person who was not a member of Democratic Action or COPEI to win a democratic presidential election in Venezuela. The first thing the president-elect did was call a press conference. Dressed in a suit and tie, Chávez cited Simón Bolívar and dubbed himself "a drop of water in a running river." Calmly, he asked Venezuelans "not to fear," promising he would not institute a dictatorship, like his opponents claimed: "It is clear from the facts that this is a lie." He also addressed the people who hadn't voted for him, calling for unity and saying, "Chávez is the national sentiment."

Chávez left the press conference for a meeting on the outskirts of the Ateneo de Caracas, where a large crowd had been awaiting him for hours. Many of them wore the signature red beret that the lieutenant colonel had popularized in 1992. He struggled toward the flag-draped dais as people showered him with hugs every step of the way. Even though he had security and was flanked by political leaders, Chávez seemed to enjoy his proximity to the people. He smiled nonstop and reciprocated any and all displays of affection. He removed his jacket as he drew near the dais, and when he reached it, took off his tie and threw it into the crowd. Now dressed more informally, Chávez—who was a natural orator—started singing the national anthem, which he followed with a speech freighted with patriotism and promises of a new nation.

Mamá was moved as she watched everything on TV. "Chávez, amigo, el pueblo está contigo," the crowd was chanting. *Chávez, friend, the people are with you.* For a country that felt betrayed by their political leaders, this was an exciting moment.

Chávez had won with 3.7 million votes in a country of 11 million voters, 56 percent of the voters who went out to the polls. Although he stirred people's emotions and restored faith in politics for people like my mother, he did not mobilize voters en masse. The abstention rate was 36.5 percent, the second worst for a presidential election in forty years.

A few days later, after sharing a flight from Havana to Caracas with Chávez, the Colombian author Gabriel García Márquez wrote "The Enigma of the Two Chávezes." He ended the article by saying that he was left feeling like he'd spoken with two different men: "One to whom luck had offered the opportunity to save his country. And the other, an illusionist, who could go down in history as just one more despot."[6]

Chávez took office in 1999 and dedicated his first few months in power to holding elections aimed at transforming the country's legal and political structure, riding the coattails of his widespread popularity. In parallel, he announced a "civil-military alliance," meaning that soldiers would leave the barracks to engage in civilian work, such as painting sidewalks or helping in public facilities. At first sight, this may not have seemed significant, but over time he increased military presence in the government, highlighting his distrust of civilians in the public sector.

---

6   Gabriel García Márquez, trans. Rob Orchard and Lluis Vilasori, "When Gabriel García Márquez Met Hugo Chávez," *Delayed Gratification*, March 5, 2013, https://www.slow-journalism.com/from-the-archive/when-gabriel-garcia-marquez-met-hugo-chavez.

Focused on the reform he had promised during his campaign, Chávez and a small committee of politicians and intellectuals designed a scheme to bypass Congress, which was then bicameral, and propose a new constitution within his first year of government.

We didn't need a new constitution—our priorities were economic and social—but what people like my mother had voted for wasn't a government. The people who elected Chávez had voted for a savior. For them, this vote was also payback against the establishment politicians who had neglected them for years. There was rage and resentment against our political parties and our democracy—what better exit strategy than rebuilding everything from the ground up?

Having popular support, Chávez called for a referendum and then for a vote to choose who would write the new constitution. The government wrapped up the plan with a mathematically infallible electoral strategy that left us with a constituent assembly that was 93 percent pro-Chávez. That constituent assembly, into which even his wife was elected, in all its intellectual homogeneity, drafted a new constitution in three months. The document extended the powers of the executive, establishing a political system in which the president—then Chávez—had few limitations. Some other adjustments included extending the presidential term and allowing for immediate reelection. But certain changes also went much deeper. The entire transition process to the new constitution was coordinated by a Chavista "congresillo," or "little congress," derived from and governed by the constituent assembly, which ultimately also named a National Electoral Council tailored to its needs. In the meantime, the head of the judiciary, threatened by Chávez, quit, calling it an act of suicide to prevent a homicide.

As a result, in the second year of Chávez's government, a number of mega-elections took place, extending the reach of Chavismo with the same electoral strategies that had been deployed for the constituent assembly.

Unlike much of the political elite of the 1990s, Chávez understood the discontent of the millions of poor people who were discriminated against, ignored, or co-opted into the country's economic machinery with no hope for social mobility, destined for a life of manual labor. The "people"—one word was enough to encompass his passionate followers—were devoted to him. He was from a poor background, like a huge percentage of the population, and had experienced these same things firsthand. Thus, the 2000 mega-election, where Venezuelans had to vote for every popular election office contemplated in the new constitution, including a new presidential election, marked the growth of Chavismo as a political force. Chávez went from winning 56.20 percent of the electorate in 1998, to 59.76 percent in 2000. But even more important than that was the fact that the MVR, the party he had founded in 1997, went from winning 22.22 percent of votes in the 1998 parliamentary elections (35 deputies and 8 senators) to 44.38 percent (sweeping 92 of the 165 seats in the recently inaugurated unicameral National Assembly) in 2000, and from 14.26 percent in the 1998 regional elections to 35.74 percent in 2000, where it closed with thirteen of the twenty-three governorships. Chávez was no longer a messiah conquering a presidential election; he was a popular politician consolidating himself, capable of catapulting anyone who helped him and sinking anyone who opposed him. His popularity was such that some politicians from opposition parties broke ranks to embrace the phenomenon and capitalize electorally.

Very few leaders of the old political elite survived the upheaval that followed Chávez's rise to power. Our democracy's strongest parties, Democratic Action and especially COPEI, crumbled little by little, and though they didn't disappear, they were never able to recapture their muscle and numbers in Congress from the previous forty years.

This became clear when, in an unforeseen twist, one of Chávez's former comrades in arms stepped up as his main rival: Francisco Arias Cárdenas, the man who'd taken over Maracaibo during the first coup in 1992 and whom my mother had fervently supported during his first foray into regional politics.

Arias Cárdenas ran against Chávez in that 2000 presidential election, and "the traitor"—as my mother now called him—was defeated in every state but mine, where he had ruled for years as governor.

Thus, in his honeymoon period, with an overwhelming constituent assembly majority, Chávez built a tailor-made political structure, strengthened his position with mega-elections, and filled most elected positions with his supporters. If there is one thing we concluded with that election it was that Chávez and political polarization were here to stay.

Chávez had started a metamorphosis, and his opponents criticized the expansion of presidential powers. With 65 percent of congressional seats occupied by his coalition, Chávez had obtained enabling powers to rule by decree. When he threatened to reform the law to get more control over the public and private education systems, his opponents reacted with protests and strikes.

Although his dissenters were not aligned—they came from different sectors and had different interests—they began to unite around the one thing they had in common: their hostility toward Chávez. Yet trying to meld so many ideologies, visions, and ambitions into a monolithic force proved to be difficult.

The country's polarization reached a boiling point in 2002.

Almost everyone in my family supported the government. Only an aunt and an uncle defended the opposition. As the two of them were clearly a minority, any political debate during family gatherings never lasted long. My brother Luis had little interest in politics, although if he had to choose, he would say, "Viva Chávez." Andrés was even more zealous about the "revolution" than my mom.

Around the time that Andrés was supposed to graduate from university, Mamá discovered he had dropped out and entered the police academy. I don't remember how we found out, but she refused to let it go. Just as she'd gone to the student union to complain that Andrés should've been in class instead of protesting, just as she'd thrown him out of the house for his behavior years before, Mamá went to the police academy and told them to fail her son.

It was a hell of an episode. Outraged, Mamá asked if Andrés had undergone a psychological screening, but she didn't wait for a response. "My son should not be allowed to carry a gun," she yelled. "And you call yourselves law enforcement officers?" There was also the classic "This is exactly why we ended up in this situation," referring to the country's problems. I stood behind her in silence. "I don't cover up for my children, which is why I'm here," she said. "If you give my son a uniform, that's on you. I've done my part. I've told you the truth." Without waiting to hear what anyone else had to say, she walked out of the academy with me trailing behind her.

Mamá hadn't been able to remove Andrés from the student movement in time to save his university career, but she did make enough of an impression on his superiors at the police academy that they rescinded his graduation.

When Mamá behaved this way, what people saw was a severity that bordered on coldness. "I want what's best for my kids, which is why I won't cover up for them. I don't want them to wind up as delinquents," she said whenever anyone criticized her ruthlessness. But it was hard to understand how she never wavered. That's another thing I tried to see in a different light as an adult. This was just how she was; it was part of her personality. It didn't mean she hated us.

My mother believed it was unwise for my brother, who so easily lost his cool, to be given a weapon. But the thing she feared the most was that, in an increasingly violent country, the bullets that had missed him during the student protests, when he had wanted to change the world, would hit him now that he'd switched sides. She was acting out of motherly love, but Andrés couldn't see that.

When Chávez won the election in 1998, the annual homicide rate in Venezuela was 20 deaths per 100,000 residents—or 4,550 cases, according to both official and nongovernmental figures. By 2002, it was almost double that.

The violence in Venezuela wasn't Chávez's handiwork, but homicide rates, which started climbing in 1989, reached unprecedented heights during his presidency. Many attributed this increase, in part, to the legalization and incorporation of new armed social factions in a country that was slowly losing its legal framework and acquiring a parallel "security" structure. The president encouraged the creation of various social organizations to serve as a foundation for his so-called revolution, a word that in Venezuela became synonymous with the Chavista movement. Among the first were the Bolivarian Circles, groups of people who came together to debate ideas taken from Bolívar's speeches and engage in community service and propaganda. Their infrastructure, which was financed by the state, proved helpful in organizing mass popular responses such as pro-government demonstrations or mobilizations to confront opposition protests. Groups like these were key during times of extreme polarization.

As Chávez lost close allies outside and inside his government, he grew emboldened. Instead of calling for discussions, he began passing more and more laws unilaterally. In 2001, using the powers to legislate by decree that were granted to him by Congress, Chávez approved a package of laws that further broadened the scope of executive authority, which especially irritated the business and oil sectors. That December, with the support of the national confederation of workers, businesspeople across the country began calling for an hours-long strike to pressure Chávez to exit. The leaders of these forces took on the role of the opposition after the official political parties had been weakened in successive elections during his turbulent mandate, now in its third year.

Tension mounted in early 2002 with increasing protests, denouncements from the business elite, isolated military leaders calling for Chávez's exit, and political parties suggesting that he be declared mentally unsound and removed from power, as well as criticisms from

PDVSA's board, which also viewed his new legislative package as threatening. The president did not back down. As the political crisis rippled into the economy, and business leaders, union workers, and former PDVSA representatives called for a forty-eight-hour strike in April, Chávez doubled down.

Frequently referred to as a "state within a state," PDVSA—the oil company Pérez created in 1976 when he nationalized the oil sector—was a state-owned entity that operated according to its own rules. Chávez wanted to change this. The oil executives challenged him, though this did not deter him. On April 7, he fired seven executives one by one on live television while blowing a whistle, as if he were a baseball coach. "Enough is enough," he said. At home, my mom applauded: "Very good! That's how it's done—with a firm hand!" she would say.

Control of PDVSA was crucial for Chávez. The company had the state's largest revenues, revenues the president needed to manage at his discretion in order to sustain his political project and finance his ever-increasing public spending.

A strike broke out in response on April 9, backed by street protests that were organized by political parties in the hope that social pressure would force Chávez to resign. Due to the importance of PDVSA in my home state, Zulia, where Venezuela's first oil well opened in 1914 and where the industry was formally established as a local symbol, people started gathering in front of the company's headquarters in Maracaibo.

Several businesses took part in the strike. As thousands of people joined protests that gained strength by the minute, private television networks broadcast images of otherwise empty streets. To counterbalance this, the government launched new television channels—which private networks were legally obligated to broadcast simultaneously—that showed images of people shopping and working as usual in Caracas and other cities, especially Maracaibo, which was ruled by the opposition and home to the oil industry. My mother and I spent most of our time at home watching the battle of the news on TV. PDVSA's headquarters were three blocks from our house, and we saw more and more people joining the demonstration against Chávez's rule. The political fight in Venezuela had also become colorful; the opposition started wearing the Venezuelan flag on their hats and clothes. They were trying to reclaim the national flag that Chávez had claimed for himself in the early years of his government, making red the official color of the revolution.

In Caracas, Chávez supporters gathered around the presidential palace in the west of the city, while his opponents were in the east. On April 11, the two sides converged and the tension exploded. The strike, which had initially been called for forty-eight hours, was now declared indefinite. With thousands of people in the streets and the support of political parties, unions, oil workers, some military, and even the church, the protest's leaders were emboldened and asked the people to march to the government palace. "To Miraflores!" shouted the hundreds of thousands of dissenters as they made their way to the presidential residence, calling for Chávez to resign—and defying the geographic division that had until then marked the political war.

My mother and I were glued to the television. Mamá gawked at the aerial images of the masses walking in Caracas, unable to believe her eyes. We had no way of knowing what was going to happen. As Chávez used an outrageous number of mandatory national broadcasts to try to dissuade the protesters, the private broadcasting channels stood up to him by splitting their screens in two, with his speech on one side and live footage of his protesters on the other. That Thursday, while Caracas was on fire, the country watched another coup unfold on live television.

Late that night, as thousands surrounded the presidential palace, and following several deadly shootings in nearby streets, Chávez peacefully stepped down from office. When we woke up the next day, we had no president and no idea what had happened the night before. With state-owned channels now in the hands of the new government, the country's private broadcasting channels reported next to nothing, until suddenly they all showed the swearing in of the new president of Venezuela: Pedro Carmona Estanga, president of the Venezuelan Federation of Chambers of Commerce. In Caracas, Chávez supporters took to the streets, and a military unit led by an old friend of Chávez's rebelled, believing a coup had forced the resignation. But it was hours before the media broadcast images of Chávez's enraged followers. Miles away from Caracas, my mother and I were shocked and confused as we followed the news. For the past few months, as Chávez used the state media for propaganda, private media sources had gradually taken up the opposition. The decision of private broadcasting channels not to equitably report what happened during those hours in April—silencing Chavismo and giving prominence to an opposition movement that had transformed into a coup—further delegitimized the Venezuelan press, whose political partiality had already sent it into a crisis of credibility.

I was in my last year of journalism school at the time. When Mamá's family gathered that Saturday over drinks, they expressed astonishment and bewilderment. They criticized the oil company's directors and the unions for allying with the businesspeople in their fight against Chávez. "Corrupt," they said. They also accused the media of supporting a coup. It was still very disorienting. Part of the armed forces supported Chávez, while another part had sided with the business leaders. The first report on the pro-Chávez protests, and on denunciations from Chavismo politicians claiming he had not resigned but was being detained in a military facility, came from the international press. There was no social media at the time, and the spread of information was slower than it is now but also safe, since thousands of Venezuelan homes had access to cable television. Chávez supporters continued to feel betrayed by the traditional parties, the banking system, the elites. Now they also felt betrayed by unions and the local media. I didn't like Chávez, but I didn't like coups either, so I listened in silence as my aunts, uncles, and mom discussed the situation, worried as they were. At twenty-one years old,

I was witnessing my third coup. The difference was that this time the president was in fact removed.

My aunt and uncle were the only ones in our family who supported the opposition, and they celebrated Chávez's departure. But that very same night, around 2:00 a.m., still gathered in my uncle's yard, we heard an announcement on the radio that Chávez was coming back. Everybody rushed to the TV, where we saw a military helicopter flying over a swarm of people in Caracas. Chávez walked out of it wearing a blue, red, and white jacket—smiling, fist raised, surrounded by followers and soldiers, and bathed in the glow of endless flashes. We still did not understand the events that had led to his release from the military facility and his return to the presidential palace. I remember how emotional Mamá and her siblings looked in that moment, on the verge of tears. Seeing her so relieved and happy made me feel good, too.

As Chávez emerged that early morning of April 14 victorious and fortified, businessman-turned-politician Carmona Estanga, and several of his allies, vacated the presidential palace.

But the country remained polarized. The secretary-general of the Organization of American States, César Gaviria, moved to Caracas to mediate a discussion between the government and its opposition. It was pointless. Chávez wouldn't back down on his authoritarian positions. He continued to push his agenda, which included concentrating power even further to weaken his political adversaries, control the Congress and Supreme Court, threaten the private media, and pass new laws on private property, education, oil, and market issues, among others.

The truth is that after April 2002, Chávez would never make another attempt to unite the country or make space for reconciliation. His revanchist discourse emboldened millions of his followers, including Mamá. Political arguments grew more intense than ever before, some even leading to divorces. When all was said and done, Chávez had been elected and now reigned over the state and the country. Anyone who disagreed could see themselves to the airport. But the opposition wouldn't back down, either. For them, the only possible outcome was Chávez's resignation.

By then my brother Luis had moved back in with us after separating from his girlfriend, who was expecting their second child. It was a painful separation for my mother, tired as she was of her eldest son's ups and downs. Still, she decided to help him. Her pension had increased over the previous few years, allowing her to set aside a bit of money. She used it to buy a refrigerator and a pair of shelves, which she installed in the back of her house, the same place where Papá had run a café two decades earlier. They opened the store just before the Christmas festivities, which in Maracaibo start in mid-November. It was the season of "gaitas," the city's traditional music, and the Feria de la Chinita, the celebration of Zulia's patron saint, which takes place on November 18. Mamá and my brother wanted to make the most of the holiday season, but just then, in what felt like an endless year, the opposition called yet another strike. Though it was supposed to last one day, the strike was extended indefinitely after renewed support from workers' unions, opposition politicians, and the media. Thousands of workers from PDVSA, including managers and senior leaders, halted operations in the oil company, impacting production and international shipments. The climax came on December 5, 2002, when the crew of an oil tanker mutinied and anchored their ship—loaded with forty-four million liters of oil—in the middle of Lake Maracaibo to comply with the nationwide strike against Chávez.

The ship was called *Pilín León*, an homage to the 1981 Miss World. The most famous brand in our country, Miss Venezuela was as much of a symbol of pride as the oil company that put food on our tables for decades. In a sort of cultural meld, a number of the state's oil tankers were named after our most successful Misses.

My mother felt resentful. The name Pilín León, a part of her national pantheon, was now tarnished. But the PDVSA workers' decision to join the strike had more than just an emotional impact. With oil operations paralyzed, our domestic fuel supply was interrupted, leaving us without gasoline and stalling commerce for months. People turned long gas lines into social hubs, bringing tables and beach chairs, playing dominoes, even drinking beer and listening to music.

We lived just a few blocks from the lake where the tanker was anchored, and our governor opposed Chávez. Even public services like our cooking gas supply were interrupted. All of this made the strike feel more extreme in Zulia. Every day, more and more people crowded near the PDVSA headquarters in Caracas and other main cities. Television channels started replacing their usual programming with news about the strike that had turned cities across the country into protest hubs, their symbol the three colors of the national flag. It was all happening again, but this time the president resisted. On December 21, El Comandante dealt a huge blow to the strike. He sent troops to take control of the *Pilín León*, which weighed anchor and docked at the port, where Chávez himself was waiting. He wanted to show his adversaries that he wouldn't go down easy. My mother celebrated the regime's victory while cursing our governor, whom she blamed for cutting off our cooking gas and making our life that much harder.

It didn't matter to us that we couldn't have a hot lunch or dinner; we could subsist on sandwiches for a few days. But we did care about our traditional Christmas meal, hallacas, stuffed corn flour tamales wrapped in banana leaves. Mamá always made them in a large cooking pot that sat across two burners, a relic of a time when Papá dreamed of opening a restaurant. She decided to use chunks of old furniture to build a bonfire, where we'd cook the hallacas, pernil, and a couple of chickens, which would have us covered for Christmas and three or four days after. Apparently, we could adapt to anything. I helped her chop up furniture with an axe that had belonged to my father.

My mother was resourceful, but she was also worried. After criticizing my father countless times for his poor business acumen, she had opened a store at the outset of a national strike, and this started to feel like terrible timing. Surprisingly, the stoppage had a positive impact on Mamá and Luis's small grocery enterprise. With everything closed, it was difficult to find food. Luis and my mother capitalized on the crisis with a tight schedule, which started with Luis sitting in line early in the morning to fuel up his car and then going to downtown Maracaibo before dawn to bring back products—mostly Colombian—that flew off the shelves of the store they ran out of our house. My mother, like a fish in water, chauffeured him and helped manage the store. If there's one thing my family knew, it was how to deal with a crisis.

The government continued to resist the labor and oil strike. Instead of calling for dialogue, they retaliated with violence. Chávez, who had gained directive control of PDVSA, fired nineteen thousand of its insurgent workers, including engineers and qualified personnel, compromising its operations. The technological unit was one of the hardest hit, its staff severely punished for being at the heart of the protest.

The strike became unsustainable, until finally it was tacitly lifted in early 2003. Soon after, Chávez appointed military officers to control several sectors of the oil company, arguing it was in the national interest. After so many layoffs, PDVSA needed to hire as many personnel as possible, and they had to do it fast. One of my cousins, an engineer only two years my senior, got a job there, achieving his professional dream. Working at PDVSA meant financial security.

That stability was taken from those employees who were abruptly fired. Some of them set up stalls and sold used wares on the same avenue where they'd protested the government months earlier. They laid out clothes, household objects, electronic appliances, magazines, and products from abroad—small relics of once-comfortable lives. The sight left an impression on me. When I was growing up, working at the oil company had always meant a life of security and abundance. Now, stripped of their benefits, those same people had to sell their possessions just to stay afloat. It must have felt like a blow to their dignity.

These changes to personnel affected PDVSA's entire operations. Many accused Chávez of choosing new hires based on their political loyalties instead of their credentials. The assertion made sense; Chávez made no bones about wanting the employees of Venezuela's most important company to be loyal to him. As the government took administrative control of PDVSA, destroying the independence the company had held on to for decades, it began to make discretionary use of the company's resources. Until then, the company had undergone regular, mandatory audits and followed formal protocols when distributing its gains. All this disappeared when Chávez took over.

For months it felt like we were waking up to breaking news and conflicts every day. Finally, in February 2003, with renewed fears of capital flight, Chávez awoke the ghost of Viernes Negro and instated an exchange control, followed by price control. In a country that imported most of its goods, access to foreign currency was once again in the hands of the government. This artificially determined the value of the bolívar, which only lost strength.

The exchange control resulted in parallel markets for the sale and purchase of US dollars. It favored corruption and the depreciation of the national currency, causing the country to develop an obsession with the American currency. Price and exchange controls altered the economy and led many producers and businesses to bankruptcy. The government decided the price supermarkets charged for basic food products, such as a kilo of rice. It also controlled access to US dollars, which shop owners needed to acquire those products. Since access was so limited—the government imposed a quota and also had other tacit requirements, like political loyalty—many shopkeepers resorted to the parallel market, paying the most expensive currency rate. This made it impossible for a kilo of rice to be sold at the government-stipulated price. Eventually this policy generated food shortages, forcing people to buy from the black market at much higher prices. The controls created a parallel economy that would suffocate the population years later.

The economy was in freefall, but the oil strike and the coup had given Chávez somebody to blame.

After the failure of the coup, stoppages, and mass protests, the opposition decided to launch a recall referendum. Ironically, the tool they were using against Chávez only existed because of the constitution approved during his first year as president in 1999. But Chávez always seemed to be one step ahead of his opponents.

As tensions mounted, the opposition started collecting the signatures they needed to activate the petition that would determine whether Chávez kept his post. Despite the country's obvious polarization, the task was an uphill battle. The government knew that the opposition would have no trouble collecting signatures and sought out bureaucratic ways to block them. To make the obstruction appear legitimate, the government counted on the newly appointed National Electoral Council, which was presided over by a man named Jorge Rodríguez, who showed signs of bias from the get-go. The council required those who had signed the petition to confirm their signatures and provide an ID, which created a database of people who were later branded "enemies of the fatherland." A deputy member of Chávez's party got hold of this database and uploaded it to the internet, allowing anyone to identify the signees by their ID number.

The portal was used as grounds for dismissals across ministries and state agencies, as well as for rescinding or blocking people from receiving state benefits that were mandated by law. It became common to hear about people losing their jobs because they had "signed." That exposition had a long-lasting impact on the national psyche. For years to come, many Venezuelans feared that their vote, which was supposed to be secret, might be revealed and lead to penalization.

It was around this time that I started an internship at a local newspaper, as a graduation requirement. By then I was so tired of the news that I was hoping to be placed in the culture section. But politics was the only beat with a spot for me. I got through it, working eight-hour days and rushing home to have "merienda," an evening snack, with Mamá. But what I really wanted to do with my time was juggle fire and crochet. I spent days—sometimes weeks, during the holidays—traveling between cities and living on whatever money I earned from performing or selling handmade necklaces and bags. Mamá hated it. I was counting down the weeks until I got my diploma so I could travel abroad and do more of the same. To me, journalism was just a degree, not a career.

It didn't help that during that time of intense polarization, the newspaper threatened to fire anyone who didn't sign the petition against Chávez. I was stunned by how much force politics had acquired in every aspect of our lives. I refused to sign in defiance of the newspaper leadership, who wound up backtracking and not firing anyone. I never told Mamá, who had despised the media since the coup of April 2002.

Mamá praised my brother Luis because he knew how to sell handkerchiefs to people who were crying, but all I got was criticism for my decisions, and this hurt me deeply. She said journalism wasn't a prestigious or lucrative career, and she hated that I spent my free time practicing juggling tricks. Things started to change between Mamá and me after her accident one morning in July 2003, when she fell in front of the house and fractured her upper femur. I was twenty-two and still living at home. When I found her on the sidewalk, she was in so much pain that I immediately called an ambulance. The health-care system had become so deteriorated that a public hospital wasn't an option. She asked to be taken to a private hospital, explaining that she had a Ministry of Education insurance policy with modest coverage. For the first time in years of doctor and ER visits, Mamá asked me to take her to a private hospital. And even there, the deterioration was apparent. The hospital was so overwhelmed that it took hours to get everything sorted out—long hours I spent by myself, because my brothers were there for barely five minutes.

Mamá went through a surgery, which didn't go as well as the doctors had hoped; she was bedridden for months. While she was in recovery, I had to take care of the house for the first time. I fed her and bathed her, cleaned the house, and did the shopping and the cooking, on top of working and finishing college. My brothers didn't help—I didn't talk to them for months—but a friend and some neighbors did stop by to offer support. Not wanting to upset Mamá any more, I gave up my dreams of joining the circus once and for all. She was proud, I think. She felt that she could count on me, even though I didn't always meet her expectations.

The experience that brought us closer was difficult and intimate. We shouldered it together, the two of us against the odds. I helped her learn how to walk again after three months of lying motionless in bed. But our burden was more than just psychological or physical. After all the challenges we'd gone through, we understood it was time to start paying for a full medical insurance plan. Mamá was about to turn sixty and had compromising illnesses. The public hospital system could no longer give her the support she deserved. We'd never needed this luxury before, but now that my mother's small pension had been padded—"thanks to Chávez," she would say—it was suddenly affordable. The president was struggling to redress the country's economy after months of political distress, especially considering the continued impact of the strike and mass layoffs on PDVSA's operations. But ever since his first years in office, Chávez had showcased a style that balanced popular social policies with authoritarianism and concentration of power. The formula proved useful for keeping his base loyal. It resonated as the work of a leader who gave to the poor while standing up to the corrupt elites who wanted to remove him from power. He needed to stay strong; his followers—like my mom—would defend him.

Chávez had managed to navigate the current in part thanks to the crude oil prices that had doubled since his ascent to power. Now that he had control of the PDVSA, he could use its revenue at his discretion.

Despite his campaign promises, public spending was not a priority in the early days of Chávez's administration, but this was going to change. Threatened by the growing popularity of the opposition—which had recovered after a disastrous year and insisted on calling a referendum despite the bureaucratic hurdles—Chávez opted for his usual quid pro quo approach.

There was social welfare in Venezuela before the revolution. We had public health and education, housing and food programs, and a retirement pension system. But Chávez realized he could use the country's oil assets, whose value continued to skyrocket, to bolster a series of programs that carried his personal seal, taking them to parts of the country that felt forgotten or neglected and therefore strengthening his base. PDVSA's income was funneled into the "Bolivarian missions," a series of social programs that Chávez created ad hoc, with no basis in the constitution. As PDVSA was transformed into a sort of social agency, its focus shifted. Instead of being reinvested in the exploration, extraction, production, and refinement of oil, its revenues would be used to finance hospitals, schools, and even small entrepreneurial investments. If Carlos Andrés Pérez had made us feel rich in the 1970s, Chávez revealed to us the true concept of an oil bonanza.

After I completed my internship and graduated from college, the newspaper gave me a small raise and I joined the staff as a political reporter, embracing a career in journalism once and for all. But at the end of the year, filled with resentment toward my brothers and tired of being responsible for everything at home, I decided to move to another city. I chose Caracas because it seemed the most obvious choice: it was far from home, there were good universities, and I was sure I could find a job there. I moved in January 2004.

The mere thought of all the political confrontations and news events we lived through during the early years of Chávez's government is exhausting. There was always something going on. Every personal or professional moment of my life during that time was in some way marked by the political crisis.

The move from Maracaibo to Caracas was no different.

The government and the opposition were staging their umpteenth confrontation in the streets. My mother, who didn't want me to leave, took me to the bus station, and just as I was about to board, the driver informed us that Caracas was in lockdown because of a protest. The bus would only set off once the National Guard had cleared the highways. My mother took this as a sign that I shouldn't go.

Sign or not, it was hard to leave. Sitting in the bus station parking lot, in the passenger seat of the car, I told Mamá that if they got the protest under control, I'd move to Caracas, and if they didn't, I'd go on living in Maracaibo. The National Guard cleared the way in under an hour. It was the first of many goodbyes.

During those days, as the price of crude oil rose, generating increased revenues for the government to use without accountability, money streamed in and a lot of people were happy, including most of my family—back to buying whiskey by the crate. What I heard at family parties when I visited Maracaibo was that this prosperity was a consequence not of the per-barrel price of oil increasing year after year, but of good management by Chávez. "That's how it's done!" they'd say. The rampant growth in oil revenue brought us back to the days of lavish spending.

Leading up to the 2004 referendum, Chávez launched eight social missions backed by PDVSA funds. Chávez's face was stamped all over the new hospitals and public clinics built under "Mission Barrio Adentro," which started with a series of clinics set up in the heart of the barrios, as the name suggests. In Venezuela, the word "barrio" refers to working-class neighborhoods. In Caracas, barrios tend to be located in the hills, where the people who migrated to the big city in search of new opportunities settled and then couldn't afford to leave, due to disparities between the cost of housing and their low salaries. Mission

Barrio Adentro expanded cooperation agreements with the government of Cuba, with whom Chávez maintained a direct relationship; he arranged for thousands of Cuban physicians to work in the program. I think this was the first time my mother voiced her disapproval of the Chávez government: she had no respect for the Cuban regime.

The idea itself wasn't bad, and the expansion of these public services was much needed. But the end goals were personal and political. The government could have improved the existing welfare system; instead, the creation of these clinics was one of the greatest expressions of the paternalism Chávez not only upheld but amplified. To this day I hear people from outside Venezuela praise the missions, and I get the feeling they think everything in Venezuela was privatized before Chávez came along. It wasn't. But until Chávez, no president had ever launched an entire parallel welfare program under their own name.

Little by little, El Comandante came to replace the idea of the state.

Chávez's public spending continued to increase as oil revenue kept growing. The state apparatus became one of the main contractors in the country, employing millions of people, many of whom were paid way above minimum wage. Despite the economic upturn, my first months in Caracas were difficult. I did not see how I benefited from the social system. With fewer opportunities in the private media, whose power had weakened, I couldn't seem to find a job. After using up my savings, I accepted the only job offer I had after six months in the capital: as a writer in the communications department of one of Chavez's social missions. That's how, around mid-2004, I started working for the government.

I spent a few months working in a mission that had been formed with the goal of lowering unemployment. In practice, however, it was the picture of administrative chaos. The only reasons the program didn't fail in its first week was the country's limitless oil income and a total lack of oversight.

The rise of the missions, which existed in a legal limbo, strengthened Chávez's relationship with the people and sent his approval rate soaring. El Comandante was the one giving them education, health, and credit to open new businesses. No one kept tabs on the missions' expenses or hiring practices. People like me were paid by the state, or through foundations and parallel payroll. I don't know if a precise breakdown exists of the money spent in these programs, which were meant to transform us in a matter of years into a fully literate country with high employment rates, strong production chains, and a flawless, wide-reaching public health system.

Though this future never arrived, by mobilizing these resources, the government was able to bring education and health care to remote areas of the country, provide technical and professional training to hundreds of people, offer microcredits to entrepreneurs, and empower the lower-middle and working classes, granting them not only resources but also recognition and the hope of progress, all of which translated into votes for Chávez.

It was in that context, with oil revenues cashing in and Chávez personally signing a parallel network of social programs, that the National Electoral Council finally agreed to accept the opposition's request for a referendum in 2004. The timing couldn't have been worse for the opposition.

Chávez's opponents approached every vote with a "this is it" mindset, thinking this election was the one they would finally win. That was how—with an all-or-nothing attitude—the fate of the country was decided. But by then Chávez had won almost every election he'd run in. It's worth noting that he secured those initial victories thanks to his overwhelming popularity.

Despite their fervor, the opposition joined the race on the recall referendum several meters behind the starting line. As in the elections that would follow, Chávez egregiously abused state resources in his electoral campaigns. With petrodollars flowing in, his defeat seemed unlikely.

There was no need for subterfuge in the voting machines; the election was simply an unequal contest.

I couldn't see clearly enough at the time to realize the mess we were in. I was convinced Chávez would lose the next presidential election and that the country would stay on course. I remember feeling tired of the endless conflict. The polarization was so extreme that it contaminated everything. I'd grown up at a time when coups were normal and political parties continuously discredited. It wasn't until that year that I felt encouraged to cast a vote.

I voted in favor of Chávez staying in power during the referendum, not because I felt an affinity for him—I never had—but because I thought the country couldn't take any more. The next presidential election would be held in two years; we could have a peaceful transition then. But I soon found out how wrong I was about my voting choice—so wrong. Two years can be a lot for a country.

"You won't be back," Chávez said on TV to the political parties that opposed him. "They won't be back," my mother repeated. Chávez won, and the millions of people who over the previous two years had taken part in a coup, mass mobilizations, futile dialogues, and various countrywide stoppages experienced their final defeat. Chávez seemed invincible.

Chapter 6

The Lord of the TV

The first question Chávez was asked after winning his first election in 1998 was how he wanted to be remembered when his term ended in 2004. According to the constitution in place at the time, presidential terms could last no longer than five years. After spending several minutes spouting phrases charged with patriotic symbolism, he turned to the journalist who had posed the question and in a humble tone said, "All I want is for the Venezuelan people to say that Hugo Chávez was an honorable man who was useful to his country."

The question was a pointed one. During that first campaign, his detractors had repeatedly brought up the authoritarian streak of the candidate who had people call him El Comandante, who became a household name because of a coup. This line of questioning appeared again and again in interviews, and although he always dismissed the fears as unfounded, his actions contradicted his words. Every step he took was for the sake of prolonging his stay in the presidential palace and concentrating more power, disguising his totalitarian takeovers as elections and his illegal maneuverings as legitimate democracy.

For example, the constituent assembly he'd promoted in 1999 as one of his first acts was tailored to his political needs, extending the presidential term to six years and allowing him to run for immediate reelection. In the history of Venezuela's democracy, no incumbent had been able to run for reelection while still in office.

Chávez even won a reset in 2000, starting his term all over again after the new constitution was approved and the country went to the national mega-elections. By the time the 2006 presidential election came around, the opposition was demoralized and divided, worn down after years of fruitlessly confronting the government in various ways. The men and women who wanted Chávez gone had not only taken to the streets in 2002, suffered the consequences of the strike in 2003, and been penalized for signing a referendum; they had also followed their leaders to the ballots in 2004 only to be told that there had been voter fraud. In the 2005 parliamentary elections, most opposition parties withdrew their candidates and asked voters to abstain, arguing that the electoral system was fraudulent. Their followers withheld their vote and watched as the National Assembly fell into the hands of Chavistas. The people were tired.

On the other hand, buoyed by oil revenues—at that point oil cost more than sixty dollars per barrel—Chávez's popularity skyrocketed, not only in Venezuela but also beyond the country's borders. For better or for worse, his name had weight in every one of the region's elections, and he used oil as a diplomatic commodity to drive international political alliances, rally people in places as far away as London, and finance projects like the TV channel Telesur, headquartered in Caracas.

Chávez's power was so arbitrary and great that a few months before his second presidential campaign, Congress authorized a change in Venezuela's coat of arms because Chávez's nine-year-old daughter found it strange that the horse in the design was gazing backward, over its shoulder, instead of galloping with its whole body oriented to the left. Then, the judiciary convicted a columnist who wrote a humorous piece about the change.

Chávez was reelected in 2006 with 62.84 percent of votes, and he decreed that his landslide win was a demand for radicalization. He would soon announce new actions allowing him to further cement his power and curtail his adversaries and even his allies. It was like every electoral victory for Chavismo was directly proportional to the level of damage he would do to our democracy. He promised to accelerate the transition to what he called "twenty-first-century socialism," a system for which he offered no clear concept and that he was modeling with his actions.

Speaking in the third person during one of his many addresses, the president described himself as "the man wielding the paintbrush, laying down and blending the colors; the artist." The never-ending revolution he started in the 1990s was a painting in progress, and as far as he was concerned, he was the only one who could finish it. He simply couldn't hand over the paintbrush before it was done—which is why in 2007, skeptical that two terms would suffice, he decided to call a referendum to reform his bespoke constitution so it would guarantee him indefinite reelections. Chávez also lined up his own allies against the wall: he announced that the revolution would not operate electorally with a coalition of parties, as had been the case until now, but with a single party: the United Socialist Party of Venezuela (PSUV), which he had founded to replace the Fifth Republic Movement, the party that had ushered him into politics. He would automatically preside over the PSUV, without anything resembling an internal electoral procedure, and any allies who were unwilling to dissolve their political parties to join his would be considered enemies. The message was clear: you were either for him or against him.

By then, I was a political reporter for the country's leading newspaper. I had quit my job at the government after a few months and secured a space as a journalist in the capital. It was not a lucrative career, but I was happy. I felt part of something. Even though I struggled through my first two years in Caracas, I managed to rent an apartment in the suburbs and in 2007 bought a small car thanks to a government-subsidized program that exempted people from paying taxes on certain models, considerably reducing its price. It was not surprising that under the new policy, Venezuela's vehicle industry reached peak sales that year.

Even though the economy was in a good place, violence continued shattering records in the first decade of the new millennium. In 2007, when Venezuela had a population of 27.6 million, 13,000 homicides were recorded, a number that would only rise in the years that followed. The government stopped talking about it, doing away with official statistics.

With the government's help, political collectives grew in number and strength, especially around the poorest barrios. Though packaged as community organizations, they were associated with violence and intimidation, and soon were viewed as armed civilian wings of Chavismo, or even paramilitary groups. In 2008, El Comandante created the Bolivarian Militia, which made it possible for any civilian to receive military training and become part of a reserve that would "complement" the armed forces should the country's sovereignty come under threat. In practice, however, they were an armed organization that could be used for social control. "The people are up in arms," Chávez said in celebration. Although his revanchist discourse had consolidated his most radical support, he lost voters who disagreed with his authoritarianism and constant references to socialism. Chávez was a divisive figure, either loved or loathed. His followers thought of him as something of a cult figure to be preserved at all costs; his detractors believed no country was possible with him at the helm. Venezuela was becoming a lawless state, in which resentment and class hatred dominated.

Chavismo was my beat. Marches, political alliances, military desertions, protests, repression, national simulcasts, roundtables, stoppages—we experienced it all in the newsroom and at home. With his charisma and political savvy, Chávez engulfed everything.

I was making my living as a journalist in a country where it was almost impossible to obtain statements, data, or answers from official bodies, and the rare times when it was possible, the information couldn't be trusted. A country where the media had become the enemy and journalists were beaten in the streets for protesting. A country where the government used its power like a sledgehammer to pressure, buy, or shut down broadcasters, radio stations, and newspapers.

But I enjoyed the life I'd chosen. I never experienced physical violence as a result of my job, which made me one of the lucky ones. I liked my routine, most of which consisted of chasing down politicians in the hallways of Congress. I don't remember any of my colleagues complaining about our day-to-day in those years, not beyond the usual. Everything we were dealing with at home, the lack of access to resources, had become normalized, and at work it was no different. Chávez's attacks on the local media, which he generally considered unfriendly, were also par for the course. His accusations and the rambling answers he gave the few times we had access to press conferences became a habit. "I'd love to, but you journalists twist everything I say," the president responded when I asked him for an interview during one of his national simulcasts.

In those days, the newspaper made us wear bulletproof vests and gas masks to cover protests, and we were required to sign liability waivers, which sent a chill down my spine. The process was illuminating. I don't know how much of what the newspaper's drivers said was true, but since we didn't have proper training back then, I heeded every word. For example, they told me not to wear my vest too tight because it could affect my breathing if the police started throwing tear gas and I had to run. I also wore a sweater over my bulletproof vest, no matter how hot it was, because they said police targeted people in vests, shooting them to break up protests.

At first I refused to wear the vest, but soon it became impossible not to. Demonstrations were part of our everyday life in Venezuela, and in the end I resigned myself to it.

I hated wearing a gas mask because it was impossible with my glasses. But the equipment is only useful if you put it on before the police start firing tear gas. I learned that the hard way. Disoriented, coughing, and unable to see because of the burning sensation in my eyes, I had to be rescued from the crowd. I also learned that I shouldn't dress in red, black, green, or white at demonstrations because at the time these colors were associated with political parties. Wearing a press ID could also be disadvantageous: Our news director supported Chávez, which could lead to harassment at opposition protests. At pro-Chávez demonstrations, being a journalist was reason enough. That is, unless you worked at a state-sponsored news channel. A comedian once said that journalists had been targeted so much that it was extremely suspicious for one not to have a prison sentence, a lawsuit, or a beating on their CV. I was a rarity.

Ministers seldom gave interviews, and when they did, they often berated us. The police and National Guard didn't think twice before harassing journalists, while deputies and government representatives were quick to sue us and our employers. Chávez used legal schemes to shut down dozens of radio stations and the oldest TV channel in the country, and he put financial pressure on newspapers by removing government advertising, something Venezuela's newspapers relied heavily on.

Nicolás Maduro, president of the National Assembly until 2006, was accessible and frequently spoke with journalists. But once his wife, Cilia Flores, took over Congress, he began closing us out, to the point of barring our entrance to the chamber. The aversion Chavista leaders felt toward journalists was immense, as was the paranoia of El Comandante, who was surrounded by layers of security whose excessive restrictions made life hell for reporters at public events.

There were no official channels for connecting with ministers and deputies, so most contact was informal. It was also a world dominated by men. This combination made it a difficult space for women to navigate. I was young and inexperienced. I never stopped to think about it—in part because there was so much happening that all we had time to do was dance to the beat that was playing. To this day, I still have trouble figuring out what was normal and what wasn't. Venezuela was falling to pieces by the minute, but I had no points of reference. I had learned how to be a journalist in Venezuela during the revolution. We could put up with anything, from the harassment to the endless hours of waiting for press conferences that never happened.

I don't really know how I managed to gain prominence as a reporter in that environment and to develop sources close to El Comandante. I guess on the one hand it was patience rewarded, and on the other, it was that someone always had something to say about someone else. Inevitably, there are veiled confrontations in power circles. And that was another challenge: trying not to become a useful tool for internal machinations between people whose only commonality was their link with Chávez. I also learned that the attitude toward the press by the men who ruled the country could be unpredictable.

After a press conference one day, two men escorted me to a car. Though I didn't understand what was going on, I knew they worked for Chávez's party, so I agreed to go with them. After driving around for a while, they parked at a military base and told me to get into another car. Inside was a politician in El Comandante's inner circle. "Didn't you say you wanted an interview? Then get in," he said before driving me through the city toward another military base. On the way, he showed me the rifle he always kept in the car because "you never know." I interviewed him while we were parked on the street. I was in my midtwenties and acting by instinct; these were the things you didn't learn in journalism school. The interview was published, just because of who the person was and the fact that he rarely gave interviews. But in the article there was no mention of how this interview had happened, which for me normalized the episode. Looking back, I realize that a big part of my job required smiling and hiding my discomfort with the informalities that made it work. Many of the deputies and ministers responded to requests for interviews less because of a sense of public duty than because they liked you. And even though this way of operating was not exclusive to Chavismo, it was with these politicians that accountability and press access became optional.

But on camera it was different, everything was scripted. Every event was an opportunity to promote the triumphs of the revolution, and Chávez was lord and master of the TV.

On top of the hour-long speeches that ran almost every day, El Comandante had a Sunday show called *Aló Presidente*, in which he sang, danced, played instruments, rebuked government, and made official announcements. He'd started with a radio program, answering phone calls from constituents—hence the title of the show. The idea was to stay connected to his voters. Later he transitioned to television and turned the program into a talk show, during which he nearly always announced some fantastic new project. Most of these projects were just facades made for TV: food manufacturing plants that never operated or infrastructure for which construction stopped after the first cornerstone. Vast quantities of money were probably wasted on these bridges to nowhere that Chávez concocted to dazzle his followers. The truth is that the reason Venezuela was more liquid in 2007 than it had been in 1998, when Chávez won the election, was the volatility of the price of oil, which was now worth more than eighty US dollars a barrel, ten times what it cost in the late 1990s.

But despite unprecedented oil revenues, the government was unable to stem inflation, which continued to rise. Chávez could not tame the economy in the authoritarian manner that he did the country's institutions, allies, and detractors. The exchange control, which established an artificial value for the bolívar, was applied with a ceiling and at political discretion, serving as a tool to threaten the entrepreneurial sector. It only served to feed corrupt currency sale schemes within the government and to boost the parallel market, in which the bolívar was freely traded at much higher values. In 2007, when the official exchange rate was in the single digits, one US dollar reached a price of more than 6,000 bolívares in the parallel market, where many private companies acquired the greenback for imports. In an attempt to disguise the real depreciation of the bolívar, the president announced the removal of three zeros from the national currency and renamed it "bolívar fuerte," which would have been funny but for the fact that it was tragic.

But politics also proved to be unpredictable for Chávez in 2007, when he experienced something he hadn't in his nine years in power: a loss. His proposal to change the constitution to allow a president to be reelected indefinitely, among other things, was rejected. But he wouldn't give up.

That year I was forced to leave the 120-square-meter apartment on the outskirts of Caracas I'd been renting with a friend for three years. Chávez destabilized the real estate market by announcing a new legal framework that purported to guarantee the right to housing but was in essence just populist rhetoric. The new real estate laws targeted private property owners—or as Chávez called them, "the oligarchs"—by making evictions for nonpayment almost impossible. While on the surface the goal of these laws was social justice, in reality some tenants took advantage of them by refusing to pay their rent, under government protection, and threatening the property owners with expropriation. As a result, rental supply fell dramatically.

This was how I found myself without a place to live at the peak of my career. My landlords were afraid of losing their properties because of the government's housing policies, under which private property owners confronted by their renters had no rights under the law.

On the east side of the city, people were renting apartments and houses only to expats for dollars, despite the fact that foreign-currency transactions had been banned since the institution of exchange control in 2003. Not only did these clients have the wherewithal to pay—thanks to the increasingly ridiculous parallel-market exchange rate—but also, being foreigners, they wouldn't try to seize property from their owners.

I stayed with friends for four months before finally tracking down a tiny room in an old house in the city center, the same area Papá had settled in when he first moved to Venezuela. The house was just around the block from where he and his family had lived for decades. Once overflowing with cafés and Spanish taverns, the neighborhood was now dark and dangerous. The wealthier neighbors paid police officers to work surveillance a few hours every night. To Mamá, I seemed to be moving backward instead of forward, which was something she just couldn't understand. In Maracaibo, my cousins and brothers didn't have to worry about rent. They all owned their own homes. Caracas was known for its poverty and the hillside slums that circled the city; it was also known as a place where outsiders lived either on the outskirts or in small rooms in the center or east side of the city. I can't count the number of times I heard Mamá say, "I don't understand why you insist on living like this." I wasn't insisting. I was just trying to stay afloat in a career that seemed to have no future, in a country where private initiative, freedom of speech, and government accountability were nonexistent.

Chávez also started expropriating businesses, farms, factories, banks, and private property. The president viewed businesspeople as his enemies and claimed to have no choice but to put their properties "at the service of the nation." In practice, the government—which used the oil surplus to compensate proprietors who were unilaterally stripped of their belongings—was wrecking the already-debilitated national supply chain. Once-successful businesses that entered government hands were either mismanaged into oblivion or willfully destroyed.

Chávez called for another constitutional referendum. This time, to boost his campaign, he proposed making all elected officials eligible for indefinite reelection—giving mayors, governors, and deputies a reason to get fully involved in the effort. The referendum passed in 2009. Chávez tailored the constitution even more to his wishes, and Venezuelan democracy continued to lose.

Mamá's salary kept increasing. Thanks to the government's tax-free program to help people purchase cars, she traded in her relatively new Chevy for another one, the most expensive car she'd ever had: a sedan with leather seats and a satellite phone. Luis, on the other hand, had decided to leave the country for what we concluded were personal reasons. He sold the food store—well established by then—to Andrés, who saw it as a good opportunity to capitalize on the prosperous moment.

Though people were happy that money was coming in—and going far thanks to subsidies and social programs—in reality Chávez and his itinerant cabinet (the president changed ministers the way people change socks) were stifling the economy.

Chávez had heavily criticized previous leaders for their dependence on oil, only to exacerbate the rentier model with his own policies, whose consequences began to be felt most acutely with the scarcity of basic products such as milk, sugar, and coffee. This was surprising to me, even though I lived in a country in constant crisis.

In those days, shortages were more severe in Caracas than in Maracaibo, so my mother didn't listen when I told her I couldn't buy this thing or that. State-sponsored news had convinced her that the whole thing was just an economic war waged by businesspeople, like the president said, which was similar to what he'd said during the oil strike and the coup: the business leaders and workers were conspiring against him. But this wasn't an economic war. It was a market response to years of oppression and tight financial controls: supply decreased, prices increased, and demand grew. That was the year Andrés closed the small grocery that my mom had started in 2002, before the national strike. Luis had come back to Venezuela after less than two years abroad, but decided against running his own business, especially in light of the current circumstances.

My rent shot up in step with inflation, which increased by over 20 percent in 2009. My salary did not keep pace. By then it was clear I wouldn't be able to take another rent hike. Unless I found somewhere else to live quickly, I would be out on the street. That's when I made the untimely decision to buy an apartment. I didn't have enough money, so I had to take out a loan. In Venezuela's lopsided economic dynamics, making monthly mortgage payments was more manageable than paying rent. The timing was terrible because it coincided with Chávez's decision to nationalize nearly a dozen banks, among them my chosen mortgage lender, leaving the little money I had saved for the down payment and my credit application in limbo. Chávez was steamrolling through his nationalization process, and Mamá began to worry. Her only asset was her house, and fear of losing it was what finally made her jump the Chavismo ship.

Listing all the nationalizations and expropriations that Chávez carried out would be a task of monumental proportions. Our constitution, which El Comandante continuously reinterpreted and modified despite having overseen its creation, guaranteed a person's right to own property. But the legislature, which was dominated by Chavismo, approved a legal framework that allowed the president to seize any commercial or industrial properties he considered strategic or necessary.

Accordingly, Chávez nationalized and expropriated telecommunications, power, and oil companies, banks, mines, cement works, ranches, the food industry, production and sales operations, and other businesses. These businesses and projects were declared to be of national importance and handed out at the government's discretion. Eventually, they stopped functioning. Without the necessary oversight, the national supply chain and the industrial sector were dead and buried, as were services such as electricity and the oil industry itself.

Many of the expropriations felt random and impromptu. One of the most memorable of these took place in February 2010, during a TV broadcast, as Chávez walked through downtown Caracas with the district mayor, his colleague and former vice president Jorge Rodríguez, who had once presided over the National Electoral Council. In under a minute, on a regular Sunday episode of *Aló Presidente*, he pointed to three buildings and expropriated them all in one fell swoop. The conversation, which took place before the president had even greeted the mayor, went like this:

"What about this building?"

"Private jewelry businesses."

"Expropriated! Expropriated!"

"All right."

"And that building on the corner?"

"Commercial spaces."

"Well, [the governor] Jacqueline [Faría] was just telling me that that little house over there was where [Simón] Bolívar lived as a newlywed [. . .] and now they're businesses. Expropriated!"

"Of course, President."

"This building here, what is it?"

"Another privately owned commercial space."

"Expropriated, Mr. Mayor! Expropriated! Expropriated!"

The scene resembled the Queen of Hearts endlessly exclaiming "Off with their heads!" but Chávez was a real-life character. The next day, the owners and employees of the businesses that operated in those buildings were put out on the street.

My mother didn't think Chávez himself would come to take her house away, but she was scared that with so much legal instability, someone might start "eyeing the house." Mamá was as proud of her social class as she was of her achievements. It was one thing to put the politicians she thought of as corrupt and responsible for the national crisis up against the wall. It was another thing to do it to businesspeople, shopkeepers, and ranchers who perhaps stood with the opposition because they were rich, but still embodied the work ethic and progress she revered. She couldn't support a government that threatened to take her property only to hand it over to "bums who want everything for free." That was how my mother defined the beneficiaries of a state apparatus that, as far as she was concerned, had become corrupt after a decade of Chavismo.

That was the breaking point, and the end of my mother's dream of the new Venezuela that Chávez had promised.

She wasn't the only one in the family to abandon the cause. Little by little, all but three of my aunts became disillusioned and broke ranks.

I couldn't figure out where we had ended up as a country. Thanks to the shortages, it was getting harder to find food. Going for a walk at night was a luxury we could not afford for fear of being mugged or killed. The truth was that getting home alive, or without being robbed, was a gift. I didn't have access to my savings because they were held in a bank that had been paralyzed by expropriation, and I was afraid I might be evicted at any moment. We normalized all of that.

Unlike many of my cousins, who owned shops or worked for the government, I worked for a newspaper in the struggling private sector, and my life was at the mercy of a not-so-generous monthly paycheck. I lived hand to mouth because it was impossible to save money. Still, I didn't complain, not only because I got to make a living telling stories but also because every day was different—that was the beauty of journalism. Another upside of my work was being able to move through different circles, which I saw as a social privilege. But unable to see beyond the money, my mother grew increasingly worried. Unlike my brothers, after five years at university, I seemed to be getting poorer and poorer.

More foods became scarce as producers evaded price controls by launching alternate versions of basic items that they then sold for marked-up prices. Yellow flour and seasoned rice were virtually the same as all-purpose flour and white rice, but tweaks to the ingredients list allowed them to be sold at market value. These products could be found on shelves, but at much higher prices, which gave me less and less purchasing power.

By that time, some people had left the country, most of them middle-class professionals with family living abroad. But leaving was not an option for me. Four or five of my cousins had moved to the United States in the prior twenty years. They were making a living there, but I didn't understand how people went about leaving, or how they started over. I couldn't see the abyss that separated the current Venezuela from the country we had been ten years earlier. Aside from the social madness, there were also severe power grid problems, dropping reservoir levels, and inflation nearing 30 percent. Back then, I took home close to 3,500 bolívares a month, roughly three times the minimum wage, still 400 bolívares shy of monthly expenses for a household of one or two people. It was a terrible situation, but I don't remember seeing it that way. Even when someone pulled a gun on me outside the house where I lived, I thought, *It is what it is.* We somehow adapted to everything—the way you don't sense your hair growing, until one day you look in the mirror and realize how long it is. I didn't see it at that time, and it would be several years before I understood that my country had no future.

The bank where I had my savings and my loan request reopened a few weeks later as a state bank, and my mortgage was approved around six months after my application was submitted. This was how, at age twenty-eight, in the middle of that crazy economic situation, I bought my first home—a thirty-nine-square-meter apartment in a residential neighborhood. But by then my personal circumstances had changed, and in the end I never spent a single night there. Instead I rented it to a friend so I could pay the mortgage.

The change was that I had fallen in love like never before, and my life turned upside down when my boyfriend, a Brazilian journalist, was assigned to work in China. Out of nowhere, after only two months of dating, Fabiano surprised me by blurting out, "Come with me!" It was all or nothing. We barely knew each other. We hadn't met each other's families, and we didn't know China, but after thinking it over for a few days, I made the difficult decision to leave. Not because I thought I was done with Venezuela, but for love. When I left, I believed that one day I would move back home.

It was a well-worn story, which is something I noted at our last-minute wedding party: the fact that so many foreign journalists who came to cover the revolution married Venezuelan women. What made Fabiano and me different—all couples believe they're unique— was that we got married five hours before boarding our flight to China. When asked how long we'd been married, we always inflated the number. Because no amount of time—a day, a week, a month— could represent the kind of love we had.

Everything happened so quickly that I had to say goodbye to my mother in a parking lot. She kept my car, my books, and a few appliances. I didn't have one cent to my name. I packed two bags and gathered up Bubú, my small dog, climbed in the car with Fabiano, and said goodbye to the Caracas I'd learned to love so much. One of the last things I saw before merging onto the coastal highway that would take us to the airport was 23 de Enero, the residential complex built in the 1950s by dictator Marcos Pérez Jiménez as part of his pilot program to modernize the country. The Le Corbusier–inspired building blocks were dilapidated, their splendor long gone. Transformed by poverty, the ranchos—precarious houses built with bare blocks and tin roofs—had taken over the surrounding "cerros," or hills. Painted in vibrant colors, these residences resembled modern nativity scenes. The project that Pérez Jiménez had devised to eradicate the slums had become one.

I had just turned twenty-nine and was frightened and sad. Although part of me was excited to discover a new place and grateful to be in that car with someone I loved and who loved me back, I was also terrified about the prospect of leaving my home, my job, and the life I had built—the only life I'd ever known. I was so dedicated to my job that my boss didn't let me quit and instead gave me a sabbatical year. "If things don't work out, come back, you'll still have a job here," he told me. Knowing I had something to come back to gave me some security. Although Mamá said I was a dreamer like my father, the truth was that all the big decisions I'd made up to then had been pragmatic. This time, I was following my heart. This time, I had decided to take the plunge.

As the plane rose in the sky, I looked down at the Caribbean Sea and thought about my dad arriving in Venezuela more than six decades earlier. *I'm so lucky,* I thought. *I'm just leaving for a couple of years.*

Chapter 7

A Distant Apocalypse

In the years following my departure, I read the news reports coming out of Venezuela like they were dispatches from a distant apocalypse. I was so deeply attached to my country that it became my only topic of conversation at dinners and meetings with more experienced, well-traveled professionals. I felt displaced, but as Leonardo Padura wrote in *The Man Who Loved Dogs*, "What else can we the shipwrecked talk about but the sea?"

Venezuela was not my immediate reality anymore, and I began to feel split between countries. Because of my husband, I wanted to know more about Brazil, but I also needed to adapt to the overwhelming reality of life in China, where I felt tiny.

In Beijing, I was impressed with how big the stores and supermarkets were, and the many brands and products on their shelves. I could walk around without being scared; no one was going to point a gun at me or try to kidnap me. I could just focus on discovering a place, making friends, and finding something to keep me busy. Being abroad showed me how life could and should be different. The day-to-day was much easier in China. Without the everyday worries that consumed me in Venezuela, I could afford the luxury of spending time with my emotions.

Our situation there was privileged. We rented a nice two-bedroom apartment in a residential complex whose towers were more than twenty stories high. The complex was right next to the subway and so big it included several parks, a gym, and a small supermarket, where I went almost every afternoon to buy something for dinner. It was the nicest apartment I'd ever lived in. With time to spare, I went to the gym, walked Bubú, and experimented in the kitchen, where I discovered that, much like my father, I also loved to cook. I learned to ride a bicycle and started studying Chinese. Fabiano worked from home, which was ideal as it meant spending more time together, especially given we hardly knew each other. We ate out often, discovering restaurants in hutongs with menus that were always a surprise—most of the time we didn't even know what we were ordering. Fabiano would always come up with a plan to explore the city on weekends. Because of the language barrier, we hardly ever went to the movies and instead spent hours watching movies at home. We traveled whenever possible, and I would send my friends photos from places like Thailand, South Korea, and Japan. They were happy for me. "It's a good thing you left," they often wrote with no further details. I timidly tried to say that I needed to work, that I felt out of place. "Why are you complaining? You're not here" was a common response. Though it annoyed me in the moment, and a part of me felt misunderstood, I knew they were right.

Fabiano and I had left Venezuela with only four suitcases. And little by little we built our first home together; there was no yours or mine. Our new furniture, dishes, and paintings had no previous history.

But something was missing.

I didn't know how to be just a wife, without a career. I started a blog about my life in China; my friends were steadfast readers. I increased my Chinese class load, learned Portuguese, and wrote some news stories that were published in various outlets, while helping Fabiano with his.

I had more things than I'd ever dreamed of, as well as more financial stability, but I didn't know how to handle it. What I missed and wanted more was my career. After devoting so much of my life to it, I'd gotten married and moved to a country where I wasn't allowed to work as a journalist because of their visa restrictions. I felt useless.

Even though I wanted to talk about this with Mamá, whom I called daily, I couldn't. Venezuela and its tragedies were the subject of the day, every day.

Knowing I wasn't facing as many hardships as she was prevented me from sharing my misgivings with her. We talked about my life less and less. I felt guilty for having fun, for spending money on clothes or makeup. It hurt me to be so far away from her. I routinely came up with random excuses to call her, just so we could talk about small things. But when she answered the phone, I couldn't tell her how I felt. Even though discussing trivial stuff with Mamá was hard, it was even harder for me to open up about everything I thought was wrong with my life. Mamá had never understood my professional choices, so I couldn't expect to her to understand why I found it so frustrating to have made it to thirty without the career I'd set out to achieve.

The only subject that brought us together was Venezuela. The situation there tormented my mother. After parting ways with Chavismo, she stopped watching state media and started reading websites like DolarToday, which rose to fame for its reporting on the daily value of the bolívar against the dollar and publishing short posts that were critical of the government. Mamá was alarmed by everything she read. Sometimes she called just to tell me about some impending catastrophe, like the discovery of more than one hundred thousand tons of food rotting in state warehouses as supply shortages escalated. By that point, fanaticism, ulterior economic motives, and information vacuums were the only ways people could still justify the government's actions.

Mamá learned how to use Twitter, where she regularly boosted posts by opposition leaders or reeled off lists of problems she'd encountered in one bureaucratic process or another. Even though she didn't engage much, she also used Facebook as a source of information. Before long, she was watching news shows and interviews on YouTube. Fabiano used to joke that she stopped being a Chavista the moment I gave her a computer and upgraded her internet package. Now she finally had a host of alternatives to broadcast television, which was dominated by the government's mandatory networks.

While we agreed Chávez was running the country into the ground, my mother craved something more radical than mere elections. She spoke with such verve and animation that I was scared she'd be reckless enough to go to a protest. With her peculiar perspective, she told me she sometimes asked Andrés to take her to the occasional opposition demonstration. Andrés, now a state police officer, always said no, which offended Mamá. "Coward, that's what he is. A coward," she'd tell me over the phone. "But Mamá, he's a cop," I'd reply. "He's on the other side. If he went with you, he could lose his job." My tone made clear how obvious this was to me. But it was about more than just logistics to my brother: Andrés was devoted to the revolution. He remained convinced that the country would eventually surge forward and that the opposition was to blame for everything.

The levels of violence continued to climb. Even though Chávez had promised to tackle this problem, his government was negligent and permissive. Homicide rates shot up alongside the country's economic prosperity, while control of the prisons was handed over to the criminal factions themselves. By 2010, deputies in Chávez's own party acknowledged that approximately 15 million weapons were circulating in a country with a population of 26 million. According to figures released in 2010 by the Observatorio Venezolano de Violencia—an NGO that took it upon itself to gather these statistics in response to the government's silence—2009 closed with a homicide rate of 54 per 100,000 residents (16,049 murders).[7] This figure paled in comparison to the homicide rate of 75 per 100,000 residents (a total of 19,133 murders) cited in the official National Institute of Statistics report for the same year, which was leaked to the press.[8]

Despite all this, the timeliest measure taken by the government in response to that year's growing violence was to forbid the media from reporting the data, putting an end to the newspapers' crime section—which, much like the morgue, had become too small to accommodate the daily death toll.

Having grown tired of hearing people on her roof, my mother decided to block their access by making yet another modification to the house, putting a concrete enclosure around the garage where my dad used to throw parties.

Much like the streets, the prisons—more overcrowded than ever—started reflecting a lawless country. My brother Andrés had started working as a police officer at one of the city's penitentiaries. We only talked when I visited Maracaibo, once a year. His stories were about more than a mere prison where survival of the fittest was rule of law and power vacuums were swiftly filled; they were about a place that had been forsaken by the state, a place where humanity was a luxury no one could afford.

With the deepening crisis and the uptick in violence in Venezuela, you learned to accept that your actions had consequences: If you wore something flashy, it was your fault when you were robbed. You took out your phone in the middle of the street? What did you think was going to happen? You had your window rolled down in the car? Be grateful

7   Yolanda Valery, "El debate por la violencia en Venezuela," BBC Mundo, August 24, 2010, https://www.bbc.com/mundo/america_latina/2010/08/100823_venezuela_violencia_debate_medios_lav.

8   Agencia EFE, "Revelan que en el 2009 hubo: 19.133 asesinatos en Venezuela," El País, August 29, 2010, https://www.elpais.com.co/mundo/revelan-que-en-el-2009-hubo-19-133-asesinatos-en-venezuela.html.

that all they did was rob you. Frankly, it could have been worse. People understood that they were responsible for their own safety, and many police officers made security into a business. It became standard for them to be hired to look after commercial establishments, as well as private residences and entire blocks where they sat in makeshift sentry boxes. Their uniforms and weapons were a double-edged sword, giving them the impunity to do whatever they wanted while also turning them into targets. My mother got increasingly worried about Andrés at a time when gang violence was an everyday thing.

Most of the police force in Venezuela was underpaid and underprepared. Many officers lived in the same barrios as the people they terrorized, with no buffer between them. They were also overwhelmed during protests. Maybe the institutionalization of corruption in Venezuela was a survival mechanism, or maybe it was an expression of who we really were as a country—a lawless place where no one trusted each other. If someone tried to break into your home, your first instinct was to call the police, sure, because the sirens scared off the intruders—but if you came across a patrol car on the street, especially at night, what you felt was fear, not faith. If the police are the ones doing the robbing and kidnapping, who can we turn to? In Venezuela, people learned this distrust at home, in the street, and on TV, where cops were portrayed as birds of prey, swooping in to pick at the spoils.

In an attempt to reduce the homicide rate, the government entered an off-the-record agreement with the various prison gangs, which was easier than hiding bodies. They would reduce the violence inside the system, and in return the government would look the other way, letting the gangs take control of every prison in the country.

Andrés used to tell me that when the different factions faced off, the police officers, who were constantly in and out of the prison, would wait it out in one of the cells. Their work inside was purely bureaucratic, figurative—the "pranes," or gang leaders, were the ones in charge. "You have no idea what it's like. The things we see and wish we could unsee,"

Andrés would say to me, and the look in his eyes betrayed the emotion in his words with unusual transparency. When he told me about the time he woke in his hammock to the sound of bullets ricocheting just meters away, his eyes telegraphed fear. The shots weren't the by-product of another conflict, but rather the work of prisoners in one of the watch-towers, entertaining themselves by waking up the police officers with the sound of gunfire.

On another day, the pranes decide to reorganize the space. They sent the patients with infectious illnesses to one of the towers, where they were confined without medical attention. The thought of those men rotting behind bars in the infernal Maracaibo heat, most likely without food, had an effect on me. I said they'd probably drop like flies. "Not at all. The people down below die first. The bullets get them," Andrés told me. Yet despite all the misery, he still believed in the Chávez government; he always had an excuse ready to explain anything and everything that was wrong with Venezuela.

Mamá didn't have the patience for his excuses. The moment he opened his mouth, she'd tell him to shut up.

The way we'd gotten used to living in a violent world struck me only after I left Venezuela. Brazil, for example, has significant violence, but the first time I visited Fabiano's family there, I was surprised to find that there were no security doors in the apartments. I walked out of the elevator and saw an exposed wood door with one, maybe two locks. In contrast, my mom's house had security doors at both entrances. Each door had been reinforced with three or four locks, as well as a mono-block padlock. As if that wasn't enough, Mamá also had an electric gate installed and used concrete and bars to seal off the spaces that had been open when I was a kid and had helped to aerate a house that was now dark and muggy, no matter the time of day. She added another security door between the garage and the living room in case someone managed to breach the electric gate. She also installed a triple-lock security door in the only bedroom on the second floor.

I called Mamá every day but only visited once a year, less often than she would have liked. She visited me once in Beijing. It was exciting to see her happy, proudly recounting how unintimidating she had found her first solo international trip, complete with a stopover in the United States, even though she spoke no English. She could still walk, but we rented a wheelchair so we could take her to see the Great Wall of China and tour the city with minimal effort. But neither the hutongs nor the lacquered duck nor the Forbidden City thrilled her as much as IKEA. As she filled those yellow bags, she looked like a little girl in a toy store. For the first time I felt she might be proud of me, and I found this frustrating. My mother—who had insisted so much on the importance of going to school and having a career, and never married my father—had shown no interest in my work, and yet was happy to see me married. Over the years, though, I came to see that she didn't know how I felt. I'd never told her how hard it was for me not to work, to be financially dependent on a husband. All she could see was that I lacked for nothing, had a man who loved me, and lived three blocks from IKEA. How could she not be happy for me? In her eyes, my life was a success.

She lived alone, and even though my brothers were right there in Maracaibo, they didn't take care of her. She also expected more from me than she did from them, a detail she liked to bring up as often as possible. It was hard to meet her expectations, especially from a distance. Up to that point, ours had been the classic story of a parent getting older and children who can't always be present. The problem was that the backdrop to this story was an ever-evolving, increasingly challenging Venezuela.

Fabiano was relocated to Brazil, so we left China in December 2012, just as Chávez, having won another reelection, announced that he was leaving Venezuela to undergo cancer treatment in Cuba. He had been ill for more than a year, and his campaign, according to sources, had been painstaking. "Chávez will not fail the Venezuelan people," the president promised in his last rally, before thousands of emotional listeners who stood under heavy rain for hours in the center of Caracas. "Ho, hey, Chávez is here to stay!" the crowd enthusiastically cried, chanting the words that had become the anthem of Chavismo after the 2002 coup. Soaked by the rain, the president smiled, danced, jumped. The only thing that betrayed his poor health was his swollen face.

El Comandante had been in power for fourteen years, more than any leader in the history of Venezuelan democracy, and there was no doubt he wanted to be in power for several more. The details of his illness were kept under wraps. It was particularly ironic that the man who governed by television and regularly addressed the country with hours-long speeches had kept the news of his cancer a secret. That was why his announcement had such a dramatic impact. In a national broadcast, he assured listeners that his departure was provisional, but if something were to happen, he'd be succeeded by his vice president, Nicolás Maduro.

I watched the news from São Paulo, where Venezuela felt closer not only because of the geographical proximity and the negligible time difference but because it felt culturally the same. Since I was legally entitled to work in Brazil, the minute I set foot there, I threw myself into looking for a job. I never imagined that the first major piece I would sell there as a freelancer would have Chávez as the main character.

El Comandante had returned to Caracas in February 2013, after a little more than two months in Cuba. On March 5 there were rumors swirling all over social media. Glued to my computer, I frantically scrolled Twitter for news. These spikes in tension were not uncommon in Chávez's Venezuela, but that day the country was like a roller coaster. The news came around midafternoon. Surrounded by ministers and Chavista figures, Maduro announced that the "leader of the beautiful revolution" had died at 4:25 p.m.

Chapter 8

THEY ARE NEVER GOING TO LEAVE

On March 6, 2013, Venezuela awoke to its first day without Chávez. He and his revolutionary promise had forever marked the country. My generation had come of age as he won his first election. Now, Chávez was dead. I flew to Caracas that morning from São Paulo. The bolívar was so devaluated that a round-trip flight from Brazil, even bought at the last minute, cost less than seventy dollars, a price even I could afford as an emerging freelancer.

Flying into the capital's international airport, located twenty-one kilometers from Caracas on Venezuela's central coast, is always an emotional experience. The turquoise Caribbean might be a cliché, but the connection runs deeper than its beauty, even for me, and even though I'm not from the coast. It's hard to explain the magic of that valley safeguarded by the Ávila mountain, whose green slopes are visible anywhere in the city.

That afternoon, the customs line at the airport was teeming with foreign journalists, many of whom had been correspondents during the first years of El Comandante's Bolivarian Revolution. His death was the end of a chapter.

My friends had come to Maiquetía, the small coastal city where the airport is located, to pick me up. The sight of people waiting for me at the airport reminded me that this was home. In Venezuela there was always someone waiting, whether relatives or my chosen family.

We left the Caribbean behind and took the highway from Maiquetía up to Caracas, driving through long tunnels in the infinitely green hills that encircle the valley. My friend Sergio was at the wheel. We'd taken that route—now famous for robberies and kidnappings—on many a Sunday in years past, either sick from heartbreak or nursing incurable hangovers, to eat seafood on the beach. "The sea breeze will do us good," Sergio used to say as we tried to let whatever breeze was blowing toward us remedy our mistakes in love and alcohol, operating under the same faith Mamá had in aloe's ability to cure everything. As I write these lines, hours from the sea and with none of that plant's fleshy leaves within reach, I yearn for those remedies, which were so handy and available then.

The highway into Caracas was lit up but deserted, just like the capital, whose streets were almost empty that night. We went straight to the center and then to Fuerte Tiuna, the military complex where Hugo Chávez's wake had just begun. As we got closer, we saw more cars and more people. "Chavista 4 life" was written on the back window of the car in front of us. All of a sudden, there were buses, motorcycles, police cars, and hundreds of people in red shirts—the color of the revolution. It was like the whole city had left the streets to gather there.

We got out of the car and started walking toward Los Próceres, a promenade that features monuments commemorating various chapters from several centuries of Venezuelan history, honoring our heroes and memorializing battles for independence. The wide pedestrian walkway starts with an obelisk and is flanked by long lines of lampposts that stand side by side. In the middle is a reflective pool. Interspersed along the path are fountains, sculptures, little plazas, benches, two rows of palms, and tree-filled gardens that serve as parking places for abandoned tanks and military vehicles on which children play. I only noticed them a few days later, when a colleague who'd been a war correspondent said—critically, full of pity or condescension for a country that didn't belong to him the way it did to me—that the carcasses of those vehicles reminded him of Iraq. I was surprised to hear this, considering years' worth of history classes had taught me about how our army had liberated five countries in the nineteenth century. To my mind, it was perfectly normal for children to pretend they were soldiers and play war.

Little Venezuelan flags adorned each of the lampposts, all of them lit. Cars and trucks and buses with revolutionary slogans on the windows were parked one after the other on the promenade, which on Sundays became something like a park for locals. People filed down the two-kilometer course toward the buildings by the Academia Militar.

At the halfway point of the promenade, two enormous white marble monoliths provide an overview of Venezuela's four primary battles for independence. Between them, on two black marble blocks, stand our national heroes—including, of course, Simón Bolívar. In 1987, when I was six years old, Papá took our family to Caracas for the first time. As a fan of national history, my father thought of Los Próceres as a must-see. Walking between the two black marble blocks, with the statues' eyes looming above you, is an impressive experience for an adult—and even more so for a child. You can feel the weight of history in the depiction of our army and those heroic events, which Chávez, who saw himself as Bolívar's spiritual heir, had always exalted. Chávez quoted Bolívar in every speech. His revolution, he said, was the continuation of Bolívar's work for independence from foreign threats. The president's obsession with Bolívar gave rise to all kinds of speculations and led to a bizarre chapter in 2010, when Chávez ordered the exhumation of the corpse of Bolívar, who died in 1830, to verify his cause of death. He questioned whether it was tuberculosis, as the official history says. So on national TV, Venezuelans watched a team of scientists exhume an almost two-hundred-year-old corpse to comply with Chávez's request.

The subject was also the talk of his peers. A few years later, a former Latin American president in Chávez's inner circle told me off the record that every time they met, he advised the Venezuelan president: "Chávez, less Bolívar and more economy."

As we neared the monoliths, we saw an enormous Venezuelan flag hanging between them, waving above the heads of Bolívar and his comrades in arms. The light was dazzling, as was the night sky—which, as the newspapers noted, was an unusual maroon color, a detail that helped set the scene and accentuate Chávez's mysticism.

Behind the monoliths, a barrier of orange traffic cones had been set up to block the passage of vehicles. If there's anything Venezuelans are skilled at, it's quickly capitalizing on any situation. As the wake unfolded, an improvised line of moto-taxis queued up to ferry people between the monoliths and the Academia Militar's facilities, where the body of El Comandante lay in state on a patio.

It was on this very patio that Chávez completed his military studies in 1975. As is customary, at his graduation ceremony he received a saber from the hands of the president of the republic. Ironically, the honor of handing Chávez his saber fell to Carlos Andrés Pérez, then in his first term as head of state. The same president Chávez would attempt to overthrow in 1992, during his second term. "You never know who you're working for," my mother always said.

The avenue next to the Academia's patio, with steps on either side, has for decades served as the site of military parades. Now it was overrun with endless crowds of people who had come to say goodbye to their leader. Many spent the night in the gardens, lighting candles and praying to saints at small, improvised altars. Others stood for hours to see Chávez in his coffin and say farewell, reflecting on the president's words and recounting anecdotes about him as they smiled and cried.

No Venezuelan president had died in office since the beginning of democracy in 1958. In a country whose politicians are known for living long lives, it came as a shock when Chávez died at fifty-eight.

There were no emotional or logistical precedents for his death in recent memory. His wake and burial went the same way his government had: following unconventional protocols and featuring hourly improvisations, surprise decisions, and symbolism that took the shape of patriotic speeches. The whole thing was televised.

By the time El Comandante died, all that was left of my mother's initial fervor was a deep-seated frustration. Everything had changed, and nothing had changed. She wasn't richer or more financially secure than she had been twenty years earlier. In fact, the money she'd managed to save up during our first prosperous decade under Chávez had been eaten up by the end of his reign due to a combination of devaluation and shortages that forced her to buy almost everything on the parallel market. She had sold her sedan and kept my car, which was more economical and less flashy, and therefore less enticing to thieves.

The news of Chávez's death didn't upset her. While I was in Caracas covering the funeral, we talked on the phone every day. As I listened to her criticize everything she'd once vehemently defended, I watched El Comandante's followers express their mourning in a variety of ways— the smallest gesture being to don a red T-shirt. Mamá, who used to watch the marches led by Chávez with fervor, was now made furious by the sight of thousands of people gathering to pay him homage.

I spent hours in Los Próceres talking to people who'd come from all over the country to say goodbye to Chávez. They were sad but confident that their president's legacy would live on. They said the country had problems, yes, but it wasn't his fault: it was the opposition, the oil strike, sabotage, the "economic war" that businesses had waged on him, and of course the "empire." That's what we'd started calling the United States thanks to Chávez—who, in his eagerness to set trends, had given us a nationalist vocabulary.

"They don't let him work" was a common refrain from his supporters. El Comandante had established an unbreakable emotional connection with thousands of Venezuelans the day he stood up against what they considered a corrupt and repressive democracy. The scars of Viernes Negro, the Caracazo, the Paquetazo, and the banking crisis of the 1990s were deep. Most of his mourners were poor men and women who felt seen by a president who had convinced them he cared about them and the country, that there was nothing more important than working for them and against the elites. His concept of "elites" was broad: businesspeople, politicians, and foreign ministers—the list goes on. Chávez always had a powerful enemy to blame for the country's problems. His dedication was so fierce that his followers felt as if he had died on the battlefront. Several went so far as to suggest that cancer cells had been maliciously introduced to his body. No inflation or shortage could sever their emotional bond.

Adding to their grief was the uncertainty about the future. As people wept for Chávez, they also needed to accept that life would go on, that they'd have to elect a replacement for their deceased leader, even as they believed El Comandante to be irreplaceable.

"Thieves," my mom said every time a left-wing leader showed up in Caracas to offer their sympathies. Not even Felipe, the Spanish prince whose praises she was always singing, was safe from her wrath. It wasn't that she was pleased about the death of the man she'd once idolized; she just wanted to see an end to the dream that had turned into a nightmare. But to her dismay, the revolution would outlive El Comandante.

The wake stretched on for so long that Nicolás Maduro's promotion to interim president went almost unnoticed. People continued lining up to take a last look at the face of the man we'd grown used to seeing every day in a barrage of televised speeches. Out on Los Próceres, not everyone agreed with Chávez's choice of successor, but most respected it. There was already an electioneering atmosphere, with shirts and posters promising votes to El Comandante's political heir.

This atmosphere was characteristic of Chávez's government. Elections were held all the time: new constitution, referendums, constitutional reforms, more referendums, mayors, governors, council members, and, of course, another presidential election. As soon as one voting cycle ended, the next campaign began. "An excess of democracy," said the leaders of Chavismo. It was a cynical statement. True, Chávez was extremely popular, but winning elections with the help of a biased National Electoral Council, discretional use of state resources, and the Congress and Supreme Court of Justice in his pocket was not exactly democratic.

While I watched that wave of believers file down Los Próceres, I remembered what Gabriel García Márquez had written in 1999 about meeting Chávez and feeling as if he had met two different men, the one that could "save his country," and the other "who could go down in history as just one more despot."

I had no doubt which of the two men Chávez had been for me, but as I gazed at the thousands of red-clad mourners and read the dire economic predictions—as I saw it, a clear consequence of the revolution's disastrous administrative practices—it dawned on me just how many people saw it differently, and I suspected that they would go on to feel that life had been better under Chávez. For them, his death would explain the misery to come.

After the wake, I went to Maracaibo to see my mother. Unlike in Caracas, the atmosphere in my hometown didn't appear to be mournful. Of course, Chávez's death was the topic of the moment. But in a country that lacked verifiable official information and media, many different versions of the truth—or fake news, as we call it now—emerged. Just as some supporters suspected that a powerful enemy had injected Chávez with cancer cells, his detractors believed the late president had died in Cuba in January and that his entourage had delayed the announcement to buy time. My mother was convinced of this. "He's been dead for ages; all those people do is lie," she said. The streets of Maracaibo, once a beacon of national progress, were much dirtier than I remembered. Contrary to the opinion of its proud residents, I'd never found my hometown to be especially pretty, but the impression it gave now was altogether different: the city felt abandoned. The country's supply chain had been severely impacted by Chávez's expropriations. This, added to the impossibility of acquiring foreign currency and the lack of a free price system, had led to dramatic shortages. The supermarkets with their empty shelves were just neon-lit depots with iceboxes containing a few heads of lettuce and other rotten greens. They were barely more than air-conditioned places that offered residents respite from the heat in a city that was scalding by midmorning. It wasn't hard to tell when there was food in the markets: if there was a line at the door that meant there was something for people to buy. If things out front were clear, then there was nothing for sale.

Everyone was always on the hunt. If someone walked by with a bag of toilet paper, the first thing you did was ask where they'd bought it. If there was a cluster of people in the aisles of a store, it was a sign that a particular product was about to hit the shelves and you should get in line.

People prowled the streets like dogs, trying to catch a whiff. Even though everyone had theories about how to stock up, it was starting to feel like getting hold of food was just a matter of luck. You had to be in the right place at the right time. That was why people sometimes lingered in supermarkets, even empty ones, in the hope that a box of food would materialize, because when provisions did show up, they flew off the shelves within minutes.

This uncertainty gave way to a new niche in the market, a discovery made by the young employees who used to bag groceries at the registers: personalized notification lists. Clients left their phone numbers and were notified by text when the products they needed arrived at the store. People lived their lives to the rhythm of these alerts: "rice just in, hurry, three boxes, one kilo per person"; "oil just in, one bottle per customer." This was privileged information that, much like a subscription, had to be paid for in advance.

Without these alerts, grocery shopping required tremendous amounts of time and patience. Staples like rice, chicken, or traditional corn flour used to make arepas could be acquired only after an extensive tour of various shops, and they were always rationed. The only products you'd regularly see on the supermarket shelves were nonessential, random items like plastic cups or shoe polish.

While I was in Maracaibo, I decided I might as well buy as much food for my mom as I could. But even though I spent hours upon hours in lines, by the end of the day, I had almost nothing to show for it.

Andrés sometimes guarded the state-run supermarkets but almost never alerted us when something came in, arguing that it would be dishonest to give us that advantage. My mother was furious. To her it was just another sign of her son's lack of affection. I listened in silence, baffled by his ever-changing concept of honesty.

I don't know if I was in denial, but at the time it hadn't occurred to me to bring my mother a full grocery run from Brazil. In those days, when I visited her, I packed only a few very specific things, like the protein drink Mamá needed to maintain what little muscle mass she still had at nearly seventy, or a couple of chocolates and other sweets that she never allowed herself to buy in those times of economic fragility, on the rare occasions when she could find them.

The year of Chávez's death was also the tenth anniversary of the food and currency price controls he imposed, theoretically to reorganize the economy and shield the country from capital flight and inflation. But in practice, they had caused havoc. Venezuela, thanks to an economy based almost exclusively on oil income, imported most of what it consumed. By establishing exchange controls—which defined not only the price of the US dollar in bolívares but also the amount of foreign currency Venezuelans could acquire—the government put businesses against the wall. Producers and shopkeepers saw their operations limited. To stay in business, they kept resorting to the parallel market to buy foreign currency. The parallel rate, which was considered illegal, continued to soar compared to the official rate, distorting the cost structures of companies and increasing their prices for consumers.

As the official rate hardly budged, the exchange rate on the black market followed its own ebb and flow. In early 2013, for example, at the same time that the government claimed the US dollar cost 6.3 bolívares, the parallel market dictated that the dollar be sold at 17.3.

Despite this disparity, stores had to adjust to the government-established prices for food and other basic products, which was practically impossible. So food gradually disappeared from supermarkets to be traded in illicit markets. People found out by word of mouth where to go to buy flour or rice. Needless to say, these parallel-market prices, which increased at the same rate at which the bolívar was devalued, were completely out of line with the country's salary scale. Buying those products was an option only for those who had US dollars and could sell them to friends, relatives, or acquaintances. That's why remittances began to gain strength and the US dollar became a national obsession.

The government had so far made up for this shortage thanks to the flood of petrodollars it had received from the oil boom in the second half of the previous decade. For years, the Chávez administration had used part of these revenues to import the products sold in state stores and supermarkets. But now oil prices were beginning to fall, laying bare a failed state and countless erratic economic policies.

Chávez had also promoted his frenetic nationalization policy to deal an economic blow to his adversaries and to gain access to the private production and distribution companies still operating in the country. But the result was the destruction of the country's supply chain. A few companies resisted, among them Empresas Polar, Venezuela's largest private company and a national icon, with facilities in several states and tens of thousands of employees. Its president, Lorenzo Mendoza, was the target of constant personal attacks in Chávez's speeches. Mendoza, who was seen as a good leader who was dedicated to his employees, faced thousands of inspections in his factories, expropriations of some facilities, and verbal threats. At times he altered production lines or partially closed factories due to supply shortages, but he maintained control of the company his grandfather founded in 1941 as a brewery. A "symbol of resistance and of hope," as he was described at a 2018 MIT Sloan School of Management event, Mendoza ignored calls to enter politics—some saw him as a presidential candidate—to keep leading a company that had withstood Venezuela's economic turmoil and the government's viciousness. Some believe that Empresas Polar survived the arbitrariness of Chavismo in part because of its emotional appeal and popularity among Venezuelans, as it was the producer of true national symbols such as Polar beer and Harina P.A.N., a precooked corn flour that is the key ingredient of arepas, the country's staple dish.

My mother, who was a fan of Mendoza even in her Chavista days, was now deeply irritated as she struggled to find her beloved Harina P.A.N. in supermarkets; production had decreased due to government impositions. Informal vendors—later nicknamed "bachaqueros," an homage to the "bachaco," a large ant species common in the region—hoarded Harina P.A.N. and sold it on street corners or in the city center for three times the state-sanctioned price. Seeing as I was roving supermarkets instead of spending my time in Maracaibo with her, I offered to buy from resellers as a way to get the shopping done as quickly as possible. But my mother wouldn't have it. "You've got money to spare, so you don't mind wasting it like that," she said. Accusing me of being a spendthrift like my father was a recurrent criticism.

I didn't have money to spare. I was trying to restart my career in São Paulo and had barely managed to line up any work in the past few years. In Brazil, I was being supported by Fabiano, but I had US dollars that I'd bought before traveling to Venezuela, which made it possible for me to navigate the parallel market; I could buy food without suffering the economic ramifications experienced by someone like my mother, who earned a pension equivalent to the minimum wage in bolívares.

The price of oil, which had peaked the year before, in 2013, now began to fall primarily due to supply exceeding demand. I couldn't imagine a worse scenario than needing to rush to the supermarket at the sound of someone shouting "There's chicken!" or having to spend hours in line just to buy a kilo of flour. But "things could always be worse" is a lesson that we, as a country, learned the hard way.

Chávez had financed his political projects inside and outside the country with oil, and when petroleum prices dropped—first in 2009 and then again in 2011—Venezuela, with no stable private sector to fall back on, ended up funding basically everything with petrodollars, from gasoline to services to food. The problem was that oil wasn't the only thing sinking: PDVSA was too.

System failures, no equipment maintenance, drastic decreases in production, and a complete lack of oversight at PDVSA were just some of the problems exacerbated in 2013. My cousins told me unbelievable stories about pirates entering Lake Maracaibo and attacking employees on oil derricks that were slowly being abandoned due to widespread insecurity. Things were so out of control that it didn't matter whether or not the employees worked. The heart of Venezuela's economy had ground to a halt, and the government decided to publicly shift its focus to continuing to find enemies inside the country (as in the opposition's so-called economic war) and outside (as in the US sanctions that followed the crisis). But there was no economic war. That was rhetoric, a fiction. The government was responsible for the crisis, and it kept adding fuel to the fire. Inflation, devaluation, the stagnation of the economy, drops in oil production, the collapse caused by the distortion in the price of gas, overdue payments on international agreements, and havoc in the export supply chain stemming from exchange control were only some of the consequences of the economic laboratory Chávez had been sponsoring since 1999. But his followers couldn't see this. For them, now that he was dead, everything was getting worse.

In Caracas, getting hold of manufactured goods was easier than it was in my hometown; on the other hand, in Maracaibo, fruit and vegetables weren't as scarce as they were in the capital. My mother bought them from an Andean family who grew their own food in a small town just outside the city. Every weekend they would bring a truckful of produce and set up a stand near our house—they always sold out in a matter of hours.

Mamá and I could argue over almost anything, and we never saw eye to eye when it came to spending money: she dismissed every suggestion I made. But what hurt most of all was when she accused me of having changed since I'd moved abroad. There was a clear disdain in Venezuela for people who no longer lived there, because life outside—as those inside believed—was easy. Mamá's refrain that I didn't know what it was like to live in Venezuela, didn't have to worry about the problems they experienced on a daily basis, didn't face hardships and therefore wasn't even entitled to an opinion because I had no idea what she was talking about reminded me of my father and his relationship with Spain, which I'd never understood or even tried to understand as a child. Now, whenever my mother questioned whether I was Venezuelan enough, I'd wonder if Papá would have thought about that, too.

Frustrated by the unending lines and logistical difficulties, I insisted that we'd done all we could: it was time to buy what we needed on the parallel market. But my mother refused. How could I possibly buy a chicken for this much, or a kilo of tomatoes for that much? For Mamá, it was a question of honor: she would go to the supermarket, assert her right to use the priority line—she was elderly and walked with a cane—and leave with the purchases she'd acquired at the official price. Whatever she could find.

At night, the streets were empty. Under the light of the moon, Venezuela was a no-man's-land. That year Venezuela experienced a total of 24,763 violent deaths, or 79 cases per 100,000 residents, according to the Observatorio Venezolano de Violencia.[9]

When it was time to go back to Brazil, I said goodbye to Mamá with the same sadness and frustration as always. Even though we fought and fought, when I had to leave her, tears would fall. "Don't cry. You'll make me cry, mija," she always said. "You can't cry—you don't have tears," I'd retort, making a joke that wasn't funny. Even if she was sad, Mamá could still laugh about her illness making it impossible for her to shed tears.

I don't know exactly when it happened, but it was like I'd become the mother and she the daughter. Leaving the country meant leaving her there, defenseless, exposed. It also meant losing her all over again; I lost her regularly, at every goodbye.

Meanwhile, the country was getting ready for another "now or never" moment, another decisive vote that Venezuelans would approach with the same ardor they'd brought to every election in this era of polarization.

Venezuela, a country used to a fair bit of turbulence, launched a presidential campaign immediately after Chávez's wake. The price of oil was still plummeting, and Maduro—who was not the least bit charismatic—needed a fast vote. Meanwhile, Henrique Capriles Radonski, his younger challenger, would have benefited from more time to wear out his opponent.

Maduro led a mediocre campaign, drawing extensively from state resources, which was par for the course at this point in the tournament. His attempts at charisma were a little pathetic. It was like watching

---

9   "2013—Las muertes violentas continúan aumentando," Observatorio Venezolano de Violencia, December 26, 2013, https://observatoriodeviolencia.org.ve/news/2013-las-muertes-violentas-continuan-aumentando/.

a bad, strained impression of his predecessor, whose body was now housed in some kind of mausoleum hastily built inside the military museum. The revolution was incapable of being organized, even when it came to exalting their figurehead. The most transcendent moment of Maduro's abbreviated electoral campaign took place during an official address, when he said he'd reencountered Chávez, now referred to as the "eternal Comandante," reincarnated as a bird.

My mother threw herself into campaigning on Twitter and Facebook for Capriles Radonski with the same fervor she'd once had for El Comandante. She even signed up to join the candidate's central campaign team.

A forty-year-old lawyer who had cultivated his own style, Capriles Radonski was the face of a new political generation. Over the previous decade he'd positioned himself as a moderate, distancing himself from more radical voices in the opposition in order to put himself forward as a presidential alternative. He had disputed the 2012 presidential election, in which Chávez won with a margin of 9 percent. In response, Chávez and his followers attacked him for being from an affluent family. The former mayor of a municipality in the metropolitan district of Caracas, Capriles Radonski had spent a few months in prison in 2004, when Mamá still believed in the revolution. "They won't be back," she said, celebrating Capriles Radonski's detention. Once a parrot of El Comandante's words, she was now full of praise for the lawyer on whom she'd once wished years of imprisonment in one of the country's most inhumane penitentiaries. The metamorphosis was impressive.

The election that would decide Chávez's successor was scheduled for April 14, 2013, scarcely forty days after El Comandante's death. I went back to Caracas to cover the vote again as a freelancer. The capital was tense, like it had been on every election day over the past fourteen years.

As soon as the sun set, people vanished from the sidewalks. I was surprised to see that metal detectors had been installed at the entrances of bars and restaurants across Caracas to prevent armed people from entering, because it wasn't uncommon for people to walk around with guns. Any given night could end in an argument, and any argument could end with shots fired.

All over the city, there was graffiti depicting Chávez's eyes. The leader of the revolution was now dead, but he watched from the walls—even those of state buildings like Congress's administrative towers. It was as if the government were trying to fill his absence with those vigilant gazes, which would show up out of the blue.

Despite the opposition's reservations about the electoral system, my mother and many other Venezuelans who were fed up with the revolution saw a possible victory in Capriles Radonski. Personally, I didn't see how the opposition would ever win. There may not have been any consistent evidence that the machines had been tampered with, yet the bias of most of the National Electoral Council was, by this point, screamingly obvious. For years, the government had exploited state resources and intimidated voters without suffering consequences. The electoral map had even been scandalously gerrymandered to benefit Chavismo. Jorge Rodríguez, president of the National Electoral Council from 2003 to 2006, assumed the vice presidency of Venezuela under Chávez just months after leaving that post. He and his sister Delcy went on to become some of the government's most influential figures. I couldn't picture Maduro handing over power; even if he lost, Chavismo would find a way to stay.

He won by 235,000 votes, a difference of 1.5 percent over Capriles Radonski. The opposition contested the result. There were protests and repression. It was no use. With agility, and before we knew it, Maduro was proclaimed president.

A feeling of deep frustration settled into my mother. That was the last time she voted; participating in the democratic process had stopped making sense. If before she had celebrated the revolution's endurance by citing Chávez's famous slogan, "They won't be back," now she'd say to me in a resigned voice, "Those people are never going to leave."

Chapter 9

EVERY MAN FOR HIMSELF

Hugo Chávez was so deeply rooted in our lives that he took on the force of myth. He became a dividing point in our history. Not only did his tenure mark a before and an after, but he also turned the cracks between us into schisms that sometimes seemed harder to resolve than our actual economic crisis. It wasn't just that the country was divided into Chavistas and the opposition, Bolivarians and unpatriotic schemers. The fault lines went beyond Chávez's telling of history as the privileged versus the unprivileged; they permeated everything. Those who had dollars and those who didn't, those who could get food and those who couldn't, those who left and those who stayed. Chávez had no trouble stirring up differences and dividing the country. He was dead, and his legacy certainly wasn't a land of equality. Now Venezuela had succumbed to social Darwinism. It was every man for himself.

Just like the country, Mamá deteriorated. She and the country stopped walking around the same time. The wheelchair, which she had used for emergencies, was becoming part of her everyday routine.

For years I'd been trying to convince my mother to sell her house, the one where I'd spent my childhood and teenage years. As she grew older and her illnesses started restricting her movement, her two-hundred-square-meter house seemed to double in size. We needed money to maintain the place, as well as contractors, who were never to be trusted. In my mind, the whole thing felt unsafe. I worried about how deserted her block was at night; she said I was exaggerating. One night she called me on Skype, crying because she could hear footsteps on the roof. Alone and scared, with no signal on her phone, Mamá had done the only thing she knew to do: she called me online. Law enforcement was overwhelmed—calling them wasn't an option—so I rang my brother Andrés, thinking he might be able to do something as a police officer. But he told me he couldn't leave: there had just been a shooting on his street. I had my mother on one line, crying tears of desperation, and my brother on the other, bullets ricocheting near his house.

Luis refused to move in with Mamá because he was living with a new girlfriend. Andrés, who'd stayed with her for a few short periods, couldn't be counted on. Of the three of us, he had the worst temper; to top it off, he wasn't a team player. My mother complained that he stole all the food she worked so hard to get, and that he was never willing to clean the house or help with the chores.

But she refused my pleas for her to sell. "I'm not leaving my home just so I can be uncomfortable somewhere else," she'd retort.

Even though my mother could still get around and do most of her daily chores, she couldn't carry anything heavy, including groceries, and she couldn't climb the stairs or clean the house, which meant we had to pay a housekeeper to come at least once or twice a week. This was more than just another unforeseen cost; it meant letting a stranger inside an elderly woman's home in a country where nobody trusted anyone.

But it was necessary. Housekeepers came and went, and it was hard to convince any of them to stay. Mamá wasn't exactly a walk in the park, I knew that. She was quick-tempered and expected her orders to be executed to perfection. Also, her crises of pain, which were unpredictable, always put her in a foul mood. She was an emotional roller coaster. Since Mamá was relying more and more on her wheelchair, I suggested we buy an electric one—the kind with a motor, a controller, and different speeds. But that was easier said than done.

Meanwhile, the shortages had become exacerbated. This was around the time Venezuela started making international news because of the long lines to buy toilet paper.

Mamá and I were fighting more and more over the phone, as our conversations were almost exclusively about logistics and problem-solving. Every email I wrote her was a mix of details from my daily life and reports on the current price of the dollar. In a single email, she'd tell me that she was worried about me, that she was sorry our relationship was difficult, that she felt lonely because I was so far away, and that she couldn't afford to buy chicken. Sometimes when we talked, I'd feel emboldened and tell her about this or that thing I'd written, seeking her approval. "How nice, mami," she'd say, unmoved. Then she would add, like an afterthought, "I'm very proud of you," before turning back to a logistical matter, such as adding minutes to her phone plan or dealing with the mouse she'd seen in the house the night before. Neither of us could find a way to be what the other person wanted. I think we both tried our hardest with the few tools at our disposal, but the emotional gulf between us grew.

Our to-do list grew longer, and sometimes I resented having to shoulder more and more of the responsibilities even as I was so far away. The country's defeat had underscored the emotional distance between me and my brothers, as well as the neurotic quarrels I was locked into with my mother. She was fed up with being sick and wanted me to take care of everything; I was fed up with losing a mother I loved only to be given a daughter I'd never wanted. The situation was more than either of us could handle.

My brothers were in and out of the picture. Luis, who was much more present than Andrés, had closed the store that operated out of the house a few years earlier, when he briefly decided to try his luck in another country. Unsatisfied, he'd returned, and after spending some time as a teller in a private bank, he started working in a bakery. By this time, he had three children with two women. The youngest child, also named Luis, lived in Maracaibo with his mother, Júlia, a nurse. Despite having gone through a bitter separation from my brother, Júlia maintained a good relationship with my mother. Luis's two older children lived with their mom in another city and had almost no contact with him.

Luis never went to college. He'd always worked in the service industry. He had no belongings aside from an old Mustang, and he lived with his current girlfriend. He barely had friends and never went out. For him, life meant working, dreaming big about money, and watching a movie at home at the end of the day. He was always on the lookout for the next thing, chasing rainbows in the hope of finding a pot of gold. No matter how many times he was faced with the reality of not getting rich off some fantastic idea, he still believed it was possible. He didn't waste his breath on politics, much less on arguing for argument's sake. For him life happened in the two-week periods between paychecks. I thought Luis was Mamá's favorite child, though she denied it.

Luis and I had grown apart due to past grudges and present-day behavior. I didn't even try to get closer to him, convinced my efforts would be wasted. He thought I was a bundle of emotions; I found him cold and overly pragmatic. We spoke very little, but his absence as a father was one big reason we argued. He had good days, and he had days when he was completely indifferent. Sometimes he could be attentive; other times he simply disappeared. He visited Mamá more often than Andrés did, but his presence and support were inconsistent. Working at the bakery allowed him to help Mamá with groceries. Food distribution was so unstable by then that most business owners were setting aside what little they received to sell to their employees—which is how Luis was able to get Mamá flour, bread, dairy, and deli meats in limited quantities.

But Andrés, whose volatile nature had not improved over the years, never helped out. He lived with a girlfriend in a house he'd built in a neighborhood relatively close to Mamá's. "I'd rather he didn't come," she would tell me on the phone, complaining that Andrés only visited her when he needed something, or that he yelled at her.

I asked Mamá to consider hiring someone to work for her on a permanent basis and live in the house, because it worried me to imagine her home alone at night on a street that was becoming more deserted and unsafe by the day. Though I didn't mention it, I resented her for emotionally blackmailing me for being far away; I got the feeling she wanted to punish me by putting her own life in danger. If something happened to her, she knew I would feel guilty for not being there.

And then one day, in the constant rotation of housekeepers, Luz showed up at her doorstep. She was Wayuu, and her family lived in Los Filúos, a barrio in La Guajira about twenty kilometers from the Colombian border, in the northwest corner of Venezuela. Luz had six siblings, and like many other indigenous women, she'd gone to Maracaibo to look for domestic work. The state capital was the obvious alternative to her forgotten, brown-earthed, slowly shrinking village. With no power or running water at home, Luz had lived an impoverished life. We were the same age, but there was no comparing the worlds we'd grown up in. She didn't have a partner or children, and because she lived two hours north of Maracaibo by car, it made sense for her to stay at Mamá's from Monday to Saturday. Commuting every day would have been untenable.

Mamá tried to resist, claiming she didn't have enough money to pay her. With market distortion and the proliferation of parallel economies, my mother's state pension had turned to dust. I offered to send her more money to offset the expense. By then I had an intermediary who exchanged money virtually and a triangle scheme to facilitate these transactions, which had become increasingly frequent and necessary as the bolívar continued to plummet. Even though Mamá was always blaming me for having abandoned her in Venezuela, it wasn't long before we realized that without the money I sent home, life would've been even more treacherous for her than it already was.

Things had changed so much that by the time 2013 came to a close, nearly my entire family was against the government. Among the few who still believed in the revolution were three aunts and my brother Andrés, whose endless opinions felt like they'd been plucked right out of Chávez's speeches. Mamá would get so worked up that she'd shut down discussions by screaming at her sister, "You're blind!" When I asked her to be more tolerant, she'd respond, "But how could I possibly not get upset? Don't you see she's lapping up everything those people say?"

We'd just gotten through another election cycle, this time at the municipal level. When the opposition won across several major cities, Maduro took a page out of El Comandante's playbook and placed some of the losing candidates in parallel posts to diminish the elected politicians' authority, demonstrating his unwillingness to cede power. Another thing the election made clear was that even though the opposition was becoming more cohesive, working as a united front instead of a bunch of fragmented parties, it too had lost its appeal at the polls. People were feeling disheartened after Henrique Capriles Radonski's defeat in the May presidential election, which was still being contested by some opposition leaders.

For me, the year-end holidays were especially difficult because I made a point of spending half the time with my mother in Venezuela and the other half in Brazil with my husband's family. My mom and I would cry over the phone on Christmas Eve. I missed her, and I regretted not being with her. I couldn't be in two places at the same time—but my heart was, as clichéd as that may sound. Then I traveled to Venezuela to welcome the New Year alongside Mamá and her siblings, with whiskey, Polar beers, eggnog, gossip, family anecdotes, and discussions of politics. Even though we celebrated the new year around a well-laid table, it was clear that my family was sinking in the same boat as the country. It was no easy feat to have parties like that. We had enough food to last us the week, for now. In the meantime, we kept on paddling.

We rang in 2014 at the house of my uncle Daniel, who was an engineer and my mother's favorite sibling. Despite the intense shortages, we had alcohol, pernil, chicken salad, pan de jamón—my favorite—and our traditional corn flour hallacas, which were always tastier when my mom made them (something every Venezuelan would say). The only children there were my cousins' kids, which might explain why there was less holiday cheer than there'd been when I was young. Back then, our parties were filled with children and excitement. Or maybe there really was less cheer this year overall. There also seemed to be fewer fireworks than there had been years earlier, when each of us kids had a small arsenal of bottle rockets at our disposal. This year, we sat in the backyard of my uncle's house in the northern part of the city, having drinks, listening to music, and recounting stories. We could sit there without fear of assault thanks to the high walls surrounding the house and the electric fence that topped them. It was a relief to be able to gather in the yard, in the breeze, and not inside, imprisoned in an air-conditioned room. I missed the parties Papá used to throw in front of the house when I was a child. I missed being able to set off bottle rockets on the sidewalk, something my cousins' kids couldn't do now because we couldn't risk leaving the outside door open or standing near the street.

In the past decade, Tío Daniel's upper-middle-class neighborhood had expanded thanks to huge houses like his, built for people who'd chosen to sacrifice proximity to the city center for more space. But that made the neighborhood a magnet for muggers. He and my aunt had a couple of vehicles stolen from the street, but their house was never broken into.

Even though my mother loved her younger brother, she felt he could be a bit flashy. The fact that two of his children were engineers at Petróleos de Venezuela didn't help. My uncle was understandably proud of his kids. His two eldest sons had graduated top of their class and married their college sweethearts. They'd been hired by PDVSA, bought houses in gated communities—which was not uncommon for upper-middle-class Venezuelans—and had children. What more could a father in Maracaibo want? Working for the oil company was the dream. PDVSA coddled its employees, who got hefty salaries and medical insurance and received monthly food baskets as a contractual benefit. They were set for life.

When my mother looked at her brother, she felt inferior—poorer, with children who were hard to brag about. Her eldest son was erratic, and even though he was a hard worker, he was also in his umpteenth relationship. Her second boy was a policeman, and even though he had a house, he was also a ball of pure resentment, and seemingly incapable of taking charge of his life. Then there was me, a walking frustration for her, all because I had left—first Maracaibo and then Venezuela altogether. And since my mother couldn't admit to feeling this way, she simply said that my uncle was too flashy.

Midnight on New Year's Eve, with twelve grapes in my hand to represent twelve wishes, was emotional, as always. I thought about my father, about the fact that my heart was split between Venezuela and Brazil, about how I'd have to leave again soon. Despite Mamá's wish for health while eating her grapes, this would be the last New Year's she spent upright. Her arthritis was advancing, and a few weeks later she was no longer able to walk. We still hadn't found an electric wheelchair, so Luz became even more essential; my mother couldn't take more than two steps even inside her own home. This put us in a bind—now we would have to hire someone to cover for Luz when she went to La Guajira on weekends.

I'd ask Mamá to go to physical therapy so that she could regain some mobility, or at the very least not lose what little she had left. But she didn't want to. "I won't go on my own," she said, her way of complaining that Luis wouldn't take her. "Have Luz take you," I insisted, to no avail. Unless one of her children went, she wasn't interested. "You don't understand because you don't have kids, but you're my reason to live," she told me. "How am I supposed to manage when you're so far away?" Not long after that, she decided she was done driving and sold my car.

This back-and-forth quickly dissipated the emotions of the new year. But it wasn't the only thing. In Venezuela there was not a minute of peace, as 2014 began with a murder that shocked the world. A former Miss Venezuela and her husband were attacked while waiting for a tow truck during a road trip—like the ones my father used to take with us to show us what a beautiful country we lived in. They were shot in their own car in front of their five-year-old daughter, who survived.

That same week, a student was murdered in Mérida, a city in the Andes with a strong student-protest culture. At the same time that similar protests were forming in several cities, the opposition was gaining ground in Caracas. Disheartened by their recent electoral defeat, they thought the only way forward was to head out to the streets. Leopoldo López, a former mayor who'd once been in the same party as Henrique Capriles Radonski—and a Maduro and Chávez rival—had become the face of this radical new movement. His cause? To overthrow Chavismo. Many people like my mother, who hadn't voted in the local elections that December, were reenergized. A perfect storm appeared to be forming against the government.

This is the problem with our Venezuela; it always feels like something is about to happen. By February people were back in the streets across several states. "I wish I could be out there too, instead of stuck in this wheelchair," my mother wrote in an email.

Mamá followed the demonstration, mostly on her computer, through live coverage on international news. The López-backed student protests were shared around the world in large part because of the brutal measures the government took to repress them. By the end of that cycle of demonstrations, which lasted three months, thousands of people had been wounded and forty-three people were dead. The government accused López of inciting violence and ordered his arrest. Following several days of tension, he publicly turned himself in to the authorities. López, who was young and handsome, was wearing a white shirt and a Venezuelan flag as the officers arrested him. The image was captured live by dozens of cameras, but my mother only found out when I described the whole thing over the phone from Brazil. She had no way of knowing what was happening because cable and online coverage of the events in Caracas were blocked that day.

There were weeks of chaos and repression. The country was all over international news, which described arbitrary arrests and torture. The accounts were so harsh that it sounded like they were talking about another place altogether. It couldn't be Venezuela. True, we were used to seeing the country in shambles. But it just couldn't be possible that on top of the chaos, our government was now torturing its people in the dungeons of places like El Helicoide, a mammoth circular construction that in the mid-1900s had been built as a shopping mall—part of the plan to modernize a country full of promise.

Not only was it possible but it was happening, as I heard from friends and colleagues who still worked in Caracas. Now people were afraid of more than just petty theft. Anyone could be arrested for taking part in the protests and wind up in prison cells where bribes—first in bolívares, then in US dollars—were the only thing that could change your luck.

After months of repression, the streets cooled again and the protests stopped. In May I invited my mother to spend some time with me in

São Paulo. Since tickets were being sold in bolívares, which had depreciated drastically, I could buy flights for both her and Luz.

It was a joy to see her and have her at my home. But our differences had grown starker. My mother felt she'd been abandoned, and I no longer had the energy to convince her otherwise. I was going through my own crisis—convinced, among other things, that I wasn't going anywhere, professionally or personally.

I had gotten a steady job as an international TV producer, which I balanced with some freelance work as an assistant for foreign journalists. But I didn't feel satisfied; I wanted to write stories. I spent a lot of time alone because my husband traveled so much. I had almost no friends. I lived far from home in a city where getting around required spending hours in traffic. I missed my friends and Caracas, but it was a life that no longer existed, for me or them. As I grew insecure, I didn't know how to fill my emptiness or who to turn to. The few friends I had listened to me, but I felt guilty; compared to their problems, mine seemed like the whims of a princess. And how could I say anything to my mom? I should have opened my heart to her, but I couldn't. We spent most of that month in São Paulo fighting, which made saying goodbye all the sadder.

A few months later, I once again raised the notion of Mamá selling the house and moving into a smaller place. She was feeling more listless by the day—because of her sickness, her loneliness, the situation in Venezuela—and I was scared someone would break into her house while she and Luz were at home. My mother had advanced osteoporosis from years of taking corticosteroids; all it would take to seriously injure her was a single push.

But she refused. She didn't want to sell the house, no matter how hard it was for her to do something as simple as changing a light bulb. It cost a fortune to have anything fixed, and getting hold of any parts or tools was a herculean endeavor.

One day at dawn, she caught a man trying to break in through a second-floor window. My mother was on her own; it was Monday and Luz hadn't yet come back from her village. The robbery was foiled because the man didn't have enough time to take apart the window; he made his escape before the sun came up. But Mamá was terrified, and, at my insistence, she agreed to brick up the second-floor windows, making my childhood home look even more like a bunker.

Not even then would she hear a word about moving.

We dropped the issue momentarily because, after many months of calling stores and suppliers, Mamá finally found an electric wheelchair. One day, on her weekly round of phone calls, she was told that a store in Maracaibo had just received a model—she would have to get there as soon as possible because prices changed daily due to inflation. Since I had to transfer funds from abroad, they quoted the price they thought the wheelchair would cost in two to three days' time, when the money would hit her account in Venezuela. When my mother got to the store to purchase the coveted wheelchair, they revealed the caveat: it didn't come with a battery.

The producer of batteries for that wheelchair model, which I would later find out had been discontinued, had closed shop in Venezuela— suffocated, like many other international businesses, by the judicial instability, violence, and exchange control. I recommended that Mamá take the wheelchair home—we'd track down a battery one way or another. It sounded difficult. In fact, "difficult" had become the adjective par excellence. Everything was difficult. At the beginning of the year, the government had redoubled its control of the foreign exchange market, in the midst of an unspoken capital flight. Obsessed with obtaining US dollars, many Venezuelans saw a loophole in the previous price-control system, which implemented a preferential currency quota for tourism. Venezuelans who presented tickets to travel abroad, among other requirements, would be entitled to buy an annual quota of foreign currency at a lower rate. It became a scheme. Friends or relatives would buy several tickets, ask for their quota, and, after receiving approval, cancel most of the tickets. Only one or two of them would travel to buy the dollars and bring them back to Venezuela, where they would sell them in the parallel market for at least ten times their value.

With the new exchange system announced in 2014, the government reduced the quota of US dollars that Venezuelans traveling abroad or importing nonpriority products could buy, creating more bureaucratic hurdles to accessing foreign currency.

International airlines had not only suffered collateral damage but also been forced by the government to operate in bolívares, which made their operations unsustainable. Little by little, all of them closed their doors, leaving Venezuela practically isolated.

Medication began to run out too. By early 2015, my mother was struggling to find the corticosteroids, painkillers, vitamins, and protein supplements she took every day, even as her doctors continued to prescribe new treatments. Her condition declined with the diagnosis of tachycardia and respiratory problems. I dedicated a lot of time to figuring out a way to send my mother her pills. The number of Venezuelan migrants had grown in tandem with the deepening crisis, and with that came the proliferation of private shipping services to Venezuela, especially Caracas. The capital was always in better shape than the rest of the country. Maracaibo was another story. Anything sent by mail risked getting stolen. Yet I could almost never find any friends traveling outside of Caracas. It took creativity to find a work-around. One time a friend of mine mailed medication tucked inside a gift-wrapped doll; another time pills arrived for my mother concealed in a gutted book. Luckily, our schemes worked.

On top of the countrywide crisis, there was always some kind of conflict in my family. It's hard to know whether the drama was normal infighting or whether it was fueled by how bad things were getting in Venezuela.

By then I had found a job more in line with what I was looking for as a journalist. The catch was that it was in Uruguay. It was not an easy decision, but I accepted. My husband and I decided to alternate trips between São Paulo and Montevideo to see each other every two weeks, which didn't seem far fetched considering how much he traveled. But once I was on the plane, alone, going to a place I didn't know, I realized it had been an impulsive decision. It was hard for me to explain why I was on that plane, but I knew it was the result of sadness. In São Paulo I felt lonely and didn't see my career improving. I left looking for something, but I didn't know exactly what it was. Mamá understood it even less. If she had no idea how I felt, what could she understand?

And then, in another unexpected turn of events, Luis decided he was done with Venezuela. He moved to Panama in early 2015.

Chapter 10

How Things Are Here

Even though Luis's visits to our mother had been sporadic, it was clear that his absence left her feeling even more alone. As we still hadn't found weekend help, I asked Luz to stay every other weekend. When she couldn't, she left lunch and dinner in the fridge for Mamá to heat up while she was gone. Sometimes Andrés stopped by to see her, but he was inattentive and didn't treat her with the care she needed. Sometimes they talked and he kept her company. Other times all they did was fight.

Things had started going missing, my mother angrily told me, obliquely accusing Luz of stealing from her. I'd try to talk her down, saying it didn't make sense. Luz had been working at the house for a while and was extraordinarily patient. I was busy trying to find my mother's medicines in Uruguay and didn't have energy to argue about the missing frying pan and blender, so I promised to buy her new ones and find a way to send them to Maracaibo. But then she started to suspect that her stocks of food were also getting pilfered. I trusted Luz, but Mamá didn't even trust Andrés, her own son, whom we later found out wasn't just stealing from her but also encouraging her suspicions about Luz. Food, medications, and cleaning products had become her most prized possessions, which is why she moved the pantry into her bedroom, where she kept everything under lock and key.

To make coffee every morning, Luz had to unlock the pantry with a key; grab the coffee, milk, and sugar; prepare the hot beverage; and then take everything back to the pantry—a procedure she repeated for every meal. No amount of caution felt like enough when Mamá's provisions, which were so challenging to get, were at stake.

With shortages continuing unabated, and Maduro's popularity plummeting as parallel-market food prices increased, the government burned revenue importing food and other products from allied countries such as Bolivia or Cuba to sell at controlled prices in state-owned supermarkets, which operated in the storefronts of businesses that had been expropriated in previous years. But demand was infinitely greater than supply, and sales were rationed; in order to buy anything, it was necessary to arrive early and stand in line for hours. Still, whether you came away with something in hand was a matter of luck. There was no guarantee of anything.

Luz and my mother spent hours waiting outside these stores, which were guarded by military personnel, as my mother complained nonstop about the fact that no one respected the priority line for the elderly and disabled. Yet she continued to ignore me every time I told her it didn't make sense to stand in line for one or two items. Even in the best of cases, they couldn't buy enough groceries to last the week. It was all scraps—a small bag of flour, a handful of beans, a bar of soap. Luz would also buy whatever she could find to take back to her family in La Guajira. But the crisis was only getting worse, and she told us that sometimes she had to hand over a portion of her groceries to the raqueteros, who'd block the door to the bus that made the two-hour trip between Maracaibo and the Colombian border. The passengers had to pay this "toll" or the raqueteros wouldn't let them off the bus. Those tolls didn't prevent holdups on the road, when Luz would get robbed of both food and money.

I was scared Luz would decide not to come back one day.

With the devaluation of the bolívar, and people fighting to find food, selling the house wasn't an option anymore. Leaving the country had become a trend: more and more houses were empty and for sale. I needed to solve the weekend situation and find more help for the weekdays.

Meanwhile, in Panama City, Luis was working as an assistant bricklayer. Although he found the physical labor exhausting, it had been even more exhausting for him to have no prospects in Venezuela. I was making barely enough to pay my bills in Uruguay, but with Fabiano's support I managed to send my mother money. When Mamá asked Luis to help, he complained, claiming I was in a better financial position. It was clear that to him, Mamá's situation was my responsibility alone. I was the daughter, period.

I was working in a news agency, which was heartening—at least I was rebuilding my career—but sometimes I just wanted to scream. It was hard having everyone I loved so far away. It was sinking in that there was no way to have my loved ones close by, that you really couldn't have it all, even though "having it all" for me just meant being able to eat a meal with my mom, have a job, sleep next to my partner, and see my friends on the weekends. I could only see my loved ones through a screen. But how could I complain? Even that was a privilege.

"You don't know how things are here," Mamá would tell me, with either sadness or fury.

At this point in Venezuela, everything was in short supply. As if that weren't enough, public services were also failing. Water and power outages had never been completely unheard of in Maracaibo; one of the first big investments my mother had made in the house when I was a child was to install a water tank on the roof. But while the water supply had been sporadically rationed every other day, now it was impossible to know when water would arrive at all. My mother had grown tired of hearing people climb onto her roof to steal from her water tank, so she decided to make yet another modification to the house: moving the water tank into the garage, which was already enclosed with concrete.

We had hardly finished solving one problem when another one appeared: Mamá's hip pain intensified. As a friend of mine used to say, "It's crazy to think about how things in Venezuela can always get worse."

At this point it was impossible to even consider a public hospital. The state health system was languishing for lack of supplies and investment. Even the Ministry of Education's health-care network, which had been my mother's lifeline years ago, had suffered so much from government neglect that it was overrun by patients who couldn't afford private services.

Mamá's orthopedic surgeon, who worked in a private hospital, informed her that the prosthesis he'd put in more than a decade ago had to be replaced. It appeared that the only way to get the implant we needed was to buy it through an intermediary in yet another parallel market. The titanium prosthesis my mother needed cost approximately $2,000. No one in my family could afford it, much less my mother, whose pension didn't even cover the basics.

I had just quit my job in Montevideo because Fabiano had won a scholarship in Boston, and I was going with him to avoid extending the distance that could cost me my marriage. It was good timing, because between my severance and my last paycheck, I was able to cover the cost of the prosthesis. The surgery went well; the problems came after. Mamá's health insurance covered the medical bills, but when the orthopedic surgeon who'd been treating my mother for decades learned I had paid for the prosthesis in dollars, he pressured my still-convalescent mother to deposit an extra fee in a foreign account. The anesthesiologist followed suit. He got hold of my mother's cell phone number and called her to ask for money, even though he too had already been paid by the clinic. Both men threatened her, and my mother, on bed rest, cried over the phone, scared she would lose her house, the only thing of value they could take from her. It saddened me to see her so fragile and impotent, and it was also striking to me how a man who had been almost a friend could be this cruel for a few hundred dollars.

I tried to reason with the surgeon, who'd known me since I was a kid, but there was no point—it was like he'd become a different person. I refused to pay them more money and did my best to reassure my mother that they couldn't do anything to her. Eventually they gave up, and I was forced to find another doctor for her post-op care. For days I kept thinking about them and trying to make sense of the twisted system that ruled Venezuela. The country was falling to pieces, and so were we.

Nicolás Maduro had been president for three years, but his popularity—which was never high to begin with—had reached a new low. This was not surprising. Inflation had hit the triple digits, and while people were living in a war zone, the president had doubled down on political repression, a defining characteristic of his government. More than fifty-eight hundred protests were held around the country in 2015, according to the Observatorio Venezolano de Violencia,[10] mostly for the people's economic rights. Dozens of protestors were arrested and thrown into the political prison, as well as other jails, accused mostly of conspiracy or treason. Throughout his fourteen years in government, Chávez had used legal subterfuge to imprison anyone he considered a threat, including his comrade Raúl Isaías Baduel, the man with whom, when still in the barracks decades earlier, he'd secretly founded the movement that led to the coup in 1992. Baduel was the only military officer behind that attempt who was not discovered and instead continued in the armed forces, reaching the rank of general.

---

10 "Conflictividad social en Venezuela en 2015," Observatorio Venezolano de Conflictividad de Social, https://www.observatoriodeconflictos. org.ve/oc/wp-content/uploads/2016/01/Conflictividad-social-en-Venezuela-2015.pdf.

He was key in fighting the 2002 coup against Chávez, leading the military operation that rescued him and returned him to power. Later appointed as the defense minister, he broke up with Chávez in 2007, expressing his opposition to the proposed constitutional reform. Less than two years later, he was arrested and accused of corruption. Even as Baduel denounced the political persecution, he remained in jail.

But in Venezuela, things are never so bad that they can't get worse. While Chávez abused his power to arrest anyone he considered a threat, Maduro's strategy of indiscriminate imprisonments was even more horrifying. They delegitimized his presidency in the eyes of the world and imposed a reign of terror on the country, where the widespread dissatisfaction was impossible to hide.

It was against this backdrop that the opposition managed to secure two-thirds of the seats in parliament in the December 2015 election, proving that the electoral road was uphill, but not impossible to conquer. For the first time, Chavismo lost control of the National Assembly—by two million votes. The government tried to overturn the results in the final hours of the year with a judicial maneuver and the collaboration of a servile supreme court.

By that point I had moved so many times in the past few years that I started to feel like someone on a reality show who was dropped in places and challenged to adjust as quickly as possible. We were living in Massachusetts and enjoying Fabiano's one-year scholarship. The only culture shock that I remember feeling was when I realized smoking was expensive and uncommon there, so I quit for good. I was fascinated by the academic life and the endless opportunities that a place like Cambridge had to offer. I understood that it was a bubble, but it felt good to be able to think and learn about other realities and perspectives. It was an experience I never imagined I would have, and it was so far from my reality, on par with traveling to Disney World as a child. I spoke with my mom every day over the phone. I hadn't seen her in nearly a year, so I was looking forward to visiting her for Christmas. Fabiano would be traveling with me.

For the first time, I decided to bring food and cleaning products to my mother. I packed my clothes in my carry-on, leaving two suitcases available for whatever fit. One ended up full of toilet paper. Soap, toothpaste, rice, beans, canned food, sugar, pasta, painkillers, vitamins, proteins, and a few items of clothing were some of the treasures in the other. I was nervous about being robbed in the Caracas airport, but luckily nothing happened, and we left to get a car, ignoring the people offering to buy "green" at the parallel-market rate while the currency exchange booths withered away without customers.

As we drove into Caracas that December, I immediately noticed the deterioration, which was glaring.

The streets were emptier than I remembered from all the hectic nights I'd spent in the capital ten years ago. Though my friends were still willing to go out, they weren't the same, or maybe I was the one who'd changed. The air was heavy. Going out meant having to face the aura of death that enveloped Venezuela: robbery and murders had long forced people to abide by a tacit curfew. Now restaurants had metal detectors and bouncers who patted down customers one by one. According to unofficial statistics, half the country was armed; people in Venezuela had been dying from gun violence for a long time.

For those who could only pay in bolívares, everything on the menu was unaffordable. For people from abroad, whose pockets were lined with dollars that grew stronger by the hour on the black market, it was hardly a sacrifice to get the next round of beer.

That night, my friends and I sat in a pizzeria on the east side of the city, where the middle and upper classes had their homes and where the opposition held their protests, because the center of Caracas—the site of government buildings, under Chavista rule—was out of bounds for anti-government demonstrations. In those days, a lot of people were still trying their best to stay in the country because starting over was so hard. In my friend group, there was only one person who'd left. Married with a young daughter, Marta left because her husband wanted to go. She wavered for a while; leaving her family was hard, and it wasn't any easier to leave the only life she knew. She left behind an apartment in the city center, on Avenida Libertador—where our group always had our meetups—as well as a car and a job, to start a new life in the United States, on the cusp of forty, making deliveries. Marta was the one who'd helped me find my last job in Caracas. We spent those years joined at the hip, years that we filed in our memories as the good days and reminisced about on the phone. Now we were more grown-up, living lives that a decade earlier we couldn't have imagined for ourselves. On the phone, Marta, who lived in New York, was always cheerful; she never complained about having to make her living driving a delivery truck, sometimes for ten-hour shifts, even though she'd been a senior political reporter before the great disaster. Nostalgia only hit us when we talked about the country we used to have; even though it was already bruised and beaten by the time we met, we never imagined it would be impossible to get back.

I'd thrown my last party in Caracas at Marta's place: birthday, wedding, and going-away party all rolled into one, hosted at "Quinta La Esmeralda." That's what we called the event hall in Marta's building—just around the corner from the PDVSA headquarters—in an ironic nod to the real Quinta La Esmeralda, the opulent locale where the Caracas elite held their own celebrations.

When you live far from home, the nostalgia comes and goes. You romanticize memories and wallow in the absences. You survive on stories, and the adage that the past is always better becomes truer by the day. Reminiscing becomes your favorite pastime. I insisted on reliving things that were dead.

Paradoxically, the bars and restaurants of the rich and famous—which we'd never frequented anyway, being neither rich nor famous—were still thriving on the terraces and streets of the city's east side. Far from leveling the playing field, the economic crisis had tilted it even more. People who had access to dollars and people who didn't—that was the division in the new Venezuela. The police repressed civilians because they could; the checkpoint soldiers scared people because they could; those who could get hold of food—subsidized or not—resold it for whatever price they wanted; those who had access to medication peddled it for dollars. Any person with an advantage used it to oppress those who had none.

The next morning, another farewell, but I didn't have time to be sad; I was nervous about checking my bags for the next leg of our trip to Maracaibo. I didn't want to be robbed at either airport. I felt like people were looking at me differently—maybe it was paranoia, but everyone seemed like a wily hunter trying to seize all the treasures I'd brought for my mother. Luckily, we made it safely to her house. When I opened the suitcase full of toilet paper, I immediately looked at my mom's face. She had a shy smile, and I felt proud. Being able to bring her provisions made me prouder than getting a byline in the *New York Times* years earlier. For her, there was certainly no comparison.

I took over the chores and let Luz have the day off because she'd talked about quitting. I also offered her another raise, which was an argument with my mom, who didn't believe Luz deserved it—they made the same amount of money, after all. It was hard to explain to Mamá that it didn't matter that her pension wasn't increasing. What mattered was that we needed Luz: losing her was out of the question. My mother was struggling to make sense of it, and I was so tired of fighting her.

In a pointless exercise, I wondered what my father would have said if he'd had to stand in line to buy rationed rice in the prosperous Caribbean country that had been his refuge from a Europe in ruins. Later that week, Andrés, who'd been working at the border for the past few months, told me that food trafficking had replaced drug trafficking because it was more lucrative. My mother, who always made a point of buying provisions in the state-subsidized markets, was finally starting to give up and acknowledge what a privilege it was to have a daughter living abroad who could bring her eighty kilos of supplies in one go and send her three or four times more money than she made in a month so that she could purchase eggs, dairy, and chicken on the black market.

I'd stopped doing the math. I didn't know what was cheap or expensive anymore. I just wanted one thing, for my mother to have food in the fridge and staples in the pantry. Though it may seem boring to talk only about groceries, that's the situation we were in. It was almost Christmas, and the only reason I didn't turn the city upside down looking for pernil was that my mother said she didn't want any pork, which is what we usually had. Even though I'd brought her as many supplies as I could, I still spent time going around to several supermarkets to stock up on food. One afternoon, we were in the living room talking and drinking coffee, like we always did, when my husband yelled "Eggs!" and pointed at the street. He'd seen someone walking by with a carton of them. I was impressed by his Pavlovian response and embarrassed not to have noticed the eggs before he did. There was no time to waste. I ran after the man and asked where he'd gotten them. Later, I came home with two cartons of eggs I'd bought from one of our neighbors. That Christmas, we had tres leches cake.

But that New Year's Eve, the party was more austere than ever. Mamá hadn't wanted to go, scared we'd be jumped on our way home. I convinced her by saying that I lived really far away and desperately needed to feel like I was part of something, surrounded by people who really knew me, my real family. Luis called from Panama shortly before midnight. No matter our past or how far we were from each other, it was hard to imagine a New Year's when we weren't hugging with grapes in our hands and listening on the radio to "Faltan cinco pa' las doce," a song about a man running home to hug his mother before midnight. I don't know if it's a Venezuelan thing or a family thing, but December 31 only had meaning when I was with my mother and her family. Without them, New Year's Eve was just another party.

My parents had always loved listening to music. Our house was quiet only when Mamá was in pain. On Christmases and New Years past, we listened to Billo's Caracas Boys, a Caribbean group that had several hits when Mamá was a kid. These songs, a symbol of her and her siblings' generation, had been the soundtrack to all our family get-togethers, especially the ones around the holidays. Their lyrics, which spoke of cities, landmarks, and various chapters of our Caribbean history, had taught me about geography, politics, and even literature. When I was a child, I used to associate those melodies with parties and cheer; these days I can't hear them without crying. All it takes is a familiar chord for me to see my mother dancing in the living room or on the patio of some relative's house, while my father nods with a Cuba libre in his hand and complains about the whiskey my uncles never shied away from buying—even back then, when we thought we were poor.

But by 2015, my mother could no longer dance, and the whiskey had stopped flowing at our family parties. We gathered at the house of my uncle Daniel, who'd gotten much skinnier and whose mobility was impaired by the same illnesses that had afflicted my mother for decades.

That year, my cousins the engineers seemed even less enthusiastic about the future of Venezuela. Uncertainty had crept into the most financially secure houses, and they were starting to think about quitting and trying to emigrate. It made me sad to hear that they, who had it all, would have to start from scratch.

Given the country's instability, my mother advised me to pay off the mortgage on my Caracas apartment, which I was still renting out. I didn't have the money to pay off a thirty-year loan, but I listened and went to the state bank that had financed it. To my surprise, when I asked for the bill, the balance due was equivalent to twenty-five dollars on the black market. The figures that appeared in the banks' systems had never been corrected to keep pace with the extreme devaluation of the bolívar, leading to losses in the millions in both credit and operations. I settled the entire debt with a single transfer. If I'd waited another six months, all I would've had to pay was one dollar.

In January 2016, Mamá and I said goodbye again. I had to get back to Boston. I cried the same tears I did every time I had to leave, felt the same knot in my chest, the same regret mixed with guilt for going back to a life without burglars or shortages while my seventy-one-year-old mother was forced to become ever more resilient.

Mamá called me shortly after I'd left. She sounded nervous. Tío Daniel had been hospitalized. While Sjögren's syndrome and arthritis weighed heavily on them both, my uncle hadn't been as disciplined about taking care of his health. A few weeks after that call, he died. His death was a huge blow for my mother—not only because she loved him but also because he was younger than she was, which made her feel like she was living on borrowed time. Mamá was terrified of death. It took me a long time to realize this, because she'd always been there to comfort me whenever I started crying out of the blue, frightened at the thought that one day we wouldn't be around anymore.

"Mija, don't be silly. Don't worry your head about those kinds of things," she'd say with a smile.

But she thought about death much more than I did. Now it was my turn to comfort her.

"Mamá, don't be silly. Don't worry your head about those kinds of things," I told her, pretending to have the level head I'd never managed to keep when it came to death.

I worried that Mamá would give in to her grief and fear of her own mortality. I was more exhausted than ever—time passed and I felt like I was running in place. I was burned out. No matter what I did, no one could convince me that I hadn't failed my mother, even though I paid lip service to people who told me, "You're doing your best." It didn't feel that way.

Around that time, I had my own encounter with the revolution's brand of social justice. I was threatened by the woman who'd been renting my apartment ever since I'd left Venezuela five years before. On social media, she supported the "end of the regime." In real life, she refused to accept any adjustments to the rent and wouldn't answer my emails or phone calls. Then she stopped paying rent completely, and at the end of the day, according to the laws of our lawless state, I was an oligarch and therefore had zero rights. Every so often I'd ask my friends for help, but they all had their own problems to deal with, and there was little they could do. "If we go to someone at the housing authority and they find out you're not in Venezuela, one of their employees will get rid of your tenant and keep the apartment for themselves," a friend warned me. I'd give up and wait a while. Then, whenever I came back to the subject, I'd hit the same wall.

A day hadn't gone by since I left Venezuela when the stress from my life there hadn't seeped into the rest of my life. Anxious by nature, I would chew over every single detail a million times, desperate for answers and plans. Those months in 2016 were no different. Because of my mother, I was neck deep in Venezuelan logic. I enjoyed academic opportunities in Boston, yet I felt like I was back at square one in my career. It was the same in my personal life: I was convinced that my marriage was slipping through my fingers. The sadness I felt was pre-emptive. It was also double edged, because even though my anxieties were real, I had food on the table—organic fruit and free-range chicken and beef—which made my worries seem absurd, and made me feel ridiculous. What right did I have to complain?

And then, we finally got some good news: a battery that fit Mamá's electric wheelchair had shown up at a factory distributor in the middle of the country. The logistical operation required to get hold of it involved several people and more than a thousand kilometers, but we managed to get the battery to Mamá, who could finally use the wheelchair she'd been storing in the house for close to a year. Scared someone would steal

155

it, she never took the wheelchair outside. Even so, those wheels changed Mamá's life, giving her autonomy within the house and freeing Luz from the exhausting combination of doing all the chores and wheeling my mother around the house, which left her no time to rest.

But getting around Maracaibo was becoming more and more complicated. The city's public transit now consisted of just a handful of buses and rusty por puesto cars, so it was out of the question for Mamá to venture out in her condition. Like food, taxis were scarcer than ever. We still had gas—"the cheapest in the world"—but the economic situation was so dire that, in February 2016, Maduro did something previously unthinkable: he hiked the price of fuel in a naive attempt to breathe new life into the economy. This was the first gas price increase under Chavismo—the first in two decades. The price of a liter of low-octane gas jumped from 0.07 bolívares to 1.0 bolívar, so filling a small tank cost 40 bolívares, or $6 USD, according to the official fixed exchange rate of 6.3 bolívares to the dollar. But at the black-market rate, which was the only one that actually mattered, a full tank cost just $1.06 USD. That made it clear how insignificant the increase was and how out of line the fuel price was. This absurd, long-overdue price hike didn't help put the state's accounts in order. The money also failed to make it into the coffers of the public transit sector, which was in decline.

At that point, the only way my mother could get around was by taxi. Yet it had become harder and harder to find a cab. Even though gas remained practically free, the lack of dollars in the industrial and commercial sectors had affected the importation of car parts. Car dealerships had started closing their doors, and automobile manufacturers were leaving the country. Changing your tire or even a car battery was now neither easy nor cheap. The disparity was such that a part could end up costing more than the car itself had a few years prior. This is how a country that had once snapped up cars—gas being a nonissue— saw its fleets fall into disuse. People sold their vehicles for parts so they could pocket some extra cash. Car bodies were put up for scrap metal, the start of another business venture. Only a handful of taxis were still operating, and it was especially hard to find one with enough room for my mother's large, heavy wheelchair. Trips to the supermarket, the doctor's office, or the pharmacy were becoming more and more difficult, particularly since it was never a matter of going to just one supermarket or pharmacy.

Whenever Mamá called a cab and told them she had a wheelchair, they'd refuse the trip. So she took matters into her own hands and had Luz push her cumbersome chair under the Maracaibo sun, covering longer and longer distances down the filthy, buckled sidewalks of a city whose ruin people had apparently accepted.

Luz was slight, but her arms were so strong, you could see the veins. They installed an umbrella on the back of the wheelchair to shield them from the white-hot sun in the city Mamá was determined to live in. Just five years earlier, she had moved around Maracaibo in a sedan with leather seats and a satellite phone. Now, wearing oversized sunglasses and a panama hat I had gotten for her, Mamá was being wheeled along nearly deserted streets in a metallic contraption by the ever-silent Luz. It was like something out of a dystopian colonial painting.

It was painful knowing that this is what it had come to just for my mother to get food, so I decided to find an alternative. A friend of mine said I should look into sending provisions to Venezuela by ship. The physical proximity of Venezuela and the US had facilitated the emergence of a prosperous maritime transportation service. The operation involved purchasing things online and squeezing them into the smallest-possible number of boxes, which were then sent to a port in Miami. From there, a ship would set sail for Maracaibo on a trip that took approximately three weeks. I was convinced that the first two boxes I sent wouldn't make it. After all, I'd been raised in a country where no one trusted anyone. When Mamá called to tell me that two boxes of medications and supplies had just arrived at her house, I was so excited; it was like I'd just discovered a magic formula. This new alternative for acquiring dry goods meant Luz only had to worry about buying things I couldn't send, like chicken or cheese.

Medication was another challenge; several of the pills my mother took required prescriptions. The pharmacies had started stocking their empty shelves with candy and other supplies that weren't on the list of controlled products and could therefore be sold at any price. It was a way for drugstores to reinvent themselves and stave off bankruptcy in the face of a scarcity of medication. Now and then, pharmacies were given boxes of basic products to sell at controlled prices, and those flew off the shelves in a matter of seconds.

Natalie, an ex of Luis's who'd remained close to Mamá even after her relationship with my brother ended, started helping us get corticosteroids through a cousin of hers who often traveled to the Colombian border.

Help of any sort was a blessing because the emotional exhaustion and sheer amount of energy needed to manage Mamá's basic needs were unsustainable. We used to spend hours on the phone discussing every detail. The most routine chores took on a titanic scale, and Mamá didn't make things any easier. She didn't understand that when she found the corticosteroids she couldn't get by without, she had to buy as many packs as possible, no matter how much they cost, because we might not be as lucky next time.

"It's too expensive. I only ordered one," she'd tell me.

"But, Mamá, you've got to sweep them all up—six, eight packs, as many as you can," I'd tell her, trying to show patience I didn't feel.

"How exactly am I supposed to pay for it? Besides, yesterday they gave me one price and today they gave me another, and that can't be right," she'd say, expressing her distrust for the whole operation.

I didn't care if they were charging us more or if the go-between was getting a cut. All I wanted was to have fewer problems, regardless of how much it cost me. Maybe it was unfair for me to tell Mamá to be patient, to complain about how stubborn she was being, but I did it anyway. We'd have the same argument over and over, and when I couldn't get her to see reason, I'd scold her, and then we'd fight and hang up. I would immediately regret it and call her back, but she'd refuse to pick up, which made me feel even guiltier. This was one of the hardest things about our fights: when my mother was angry, she wouldn't answer the phone. Even though I was always 99 percent sure she was fine, that she was just being stubborn, my head would spin out of control, and I'd become convinced that someone had broken into the house or that she was having a medical event. Then I'd fly into a panic.

People often say that Venezuelans overstate their fears. My friends from abroad complain how unpleasant it is to hear over and over that you shouldn't go out alone at night in Venezuela because something could happen. But it's hard to explain the psychological impact of violence. An abstract word and a string of murder statistics can't translate to the way I feel when I walk down a dark street or hear a noise in the dead of night. I know that violence isn't exclusive to Venezuela—there are robberies and homicides in other capital cities across Latin America—but it's not the same. Nothing is.

Brimming with anxiety, I'd call Mamá over and over until she finally picked up.

"I don't want to talk to you right now," she'd snap at me, then hang up again.

For a few seconds I'd feel reassured—nothing bad had happened. But then I'd cry out of frustration. I'd picked yet another fight with my mother, for no reason except how much her medication cost, and how many packs of it she should buy. Our relationship was too dysfunctional to survive Venezuela. Exhausted, frightened that my mother might run out of the corticosteroids she needed to manage her pain, I'd write to my brother's ex-girlfriend to ask her to purchase as many packs as she could and pretend they'd been marked down. I would make up the difference without telling Mamá.

Mamá was feeling older, more alone, and more powerless by the day. Meanwhile, I was either preoccupied with her or busy overseeing our factory of impromptu solutions for all the problems that cropped up day after day. Luis had no idea what was going on. He didn't call me, and I never asked him to take responsibility for those sorts of things because I knew he couldn't be counted on. I figured he assumed things were going amazingly for me. I didn't have the time, or maybe I didn't want to have the time, to ask how he was. I can't say I missed him, although I hadn't seen him in years. I knew almost nothing about him. It was no different with Andrés.

My mother once told me that she was so sick and medicated when she got pregnant with me that she downed a concoction to try to induce a miscarriage. As I got older, deep down I felt that I needed to pay her back for what she lost in those nine months of pregnancy. Unlike my older brothers, I'd made her weaker, and I had to make up for that somehow. I wanted her to see that the sacrifices she'd made for me hadn't been in vain. But Venezuela and the physical distance that separated us made everything more difficult.

Chapter 11

Things Didn't Work Out

All my mother's problem-solving strategies and formulas were rendered ineffective in Maduro's Venezuela. She'd managed to raise her children with modest means, while at the same time shielding us from poverty. She didn't owe anyone money and still had a house in her name. She'd made enormous progress. But now, at her most vulnerable, she was forced to navigate an inhumane, oppressive Venezuela. This crushed her, and I was starting to doubt that things could keep on working out, one way or another.

In April 2016, the government announced the creation of another basic food-basket program. The main difference from previous ones was that supplies would be delivered straight to people's houses, theoretically reducing supermarket lines. The small boxes filled with rice and flour were provided by the Local Committees for Supply and Production, popularly known as CLAPS, which is also what the boxes came to be called. Most of the items were imported from ally countries. The boxes would be sold at token prices, and their distribution overseen by the famously ineffective local committee structure created under Hugo Chávez. Much like the government's other revolutionary measures, this was just another scheme that sent money abroad and benefited those in the program's chain of command—mostly military and businesspeople. Though it was supposed to make monthly deliveries, in its first year the CLAPS truck showed up only twice at my mother's door. She told me that her first impulse was to curse them out and send them away, but then she thought better of it and gave the food baskets to Luz to take home.

Luz's family in La Guajira was in a much worse situation. Her sister was thinking of going to Colombia, where she could do the same work for more pay. Hearing that made me anxious. We hadn't even managed to find someone to look after my mother on weekends; I didn't want to think of how hard it would be to find a replacement for Luz. Mamá went back and forth on the topic. Even though most of the time she knew she'd be lost without Luz, sometimes her outrage pushed her into a logic that made no sense in the Venezuela where she lived. She questioned my decision to keep raising Luz's salary while her own income remained the same. This argument happened regularly, and often became personal. "You always take her side," my mother would complain.

I did take Luz's side, because I knew how challenging Mamá could be. It was impossible to make her happy. Getting groceries was one of the errands I most dreaded running with my mother, who could sometimes be sour, and question everyone else's ability to select fruit and vegetables. No one could choose an avocado or a papaya, her favorite fruit, like she could. When I was a kid, if my mother needed something last minute for lunch, she'd ask my father to go to the market. Even though there were two corner stores just meters from our house, we were only allowed to buy small things there, like matches. "It's too pricey," she'd say. "You think I'm paying more than what they charge at the market?" So Papá would grab the keys to his old pickup truck and go to the supermarket for a couple of tomatoes or some potatoes. "You call this a tomato?" my mother would say to him when he came home, grocery bag in hand.

Luz had the patience to deal with these outbursts in times when just finding a papaya was a miracle, but I was worried these routine fights were only adding to Luz's exhaustion. Then an additional challenge arrived: the massive devaluation caused a cash crisis. Venezuelans needed more bills because the bolívar was worth less with each passing day. Because of this, wire transfers became a very popular payment method. My mother, used to cash, did her best to navigate the online banking system so she wouldn't have to rely on me to wire her money for groceries or services. But it wasn't easy. Not only because she was always forgetting her passwords as well as each step of the virtual system, but also because the website of her state-run bank was constantly down. Stores had trouble connecting too, which limited payment options and made things more expensive, as their prices increased from one hour to the next. Because of the cash shortage, ATMs had a daily limit and most of the time were out of service. Then, to get cash, my mother had no choice but to personally go to the closest state-run bank branch to retrieve her pension.

Although the government insisted Venezuela was the victim of economic warfare and international sanctions, the distortions that characterized the country's economy could be traced to decisions made during the revolution. This was a homegrown catastrophe, stamped with our national seal. Just as Chávez had done years earlier, Maduro brandished his patriotic sword against outside and internal enemies. "This is Bolívar's nation," Maduro exclaimed, in his uncharismatic speeches. Compared to the real-life situation on the streets, the president's words felt like a cruel joke. "What nation? You can't even get hold of an ID card here," my mother said when she was unable to renew her national identification document.

By that time, Luis was living in a small rented room and working as a waiter at an Italian restaurant in Panama. He was just one of thousands of Venezuelans who had recently emigrated, making the news. In Maracaibo, my mother was becoming increasingly vulnerable and needy. She told me she was more sensitive, that any little thing made her cry. This feeling of vulnerability was new for Mamá. I don't know when it happened, but I do know that in the past, she hardly cried at all. When she was upset, she either yelled or argued. It was Mamá who taught me to tamp down my emotions; the tears I cried as a child didn't move her but hardened her instead. I didn't know how to respond to her growing fragility. Luis, who'd always been detached, simply ignored her calls. But I couldn't. We wound up stuck in a cycle of pointless, exhausting fights.

I wanted to find a solution, but was convinced that the only way to solve anything started with Mamá moving somewhere safer, where there were fewer obstacles. So when she refused to leave the house, I always hit a wall.

I started to put more pressure on Luis to help out, and he began calling Mamá from time to time and sending money, but Andrés remained the emotional link no one could count on. I tried to see things from Andrés's perspective; I tried to understand him and establish a bridge. I sorely needed his help with Mamá. On those days when the burden I carried was especially heavy, I wanted my brothers to share it, whether they loved me or not. The fact is I couldn't see a way out anymore; I'd run out of tricks for solving Mamá's problems in Venezuela from thousands of kilometers away. She needed her sons, because the emotional strain made the economic difficulties even harder to bear.

Every day, the ebbs and flows of a failed economy presented her with brand-new challenges that she couldn't meet. I tried to ease her frustration. There was no point in dwelling on things, I explained. We just had to single out a problem and face it head-on.

"I'm tired, mija," Mamá would say.

Her health had continued to deteriorate with age, as expected in someone with an incurable illness. She dabbled in all kinds of treatments to manage the pain and reduce the inflammation in her joints. She also dabbled in alternative medicine to alleviate some of the effects of Sjögren's syndrome on her body. I didn't know how to handle all of that, especially when I could barely figure out how to tackle my own sadness and frustration. I called Mamá every day and wrote to her all the time, but we fought a lot. Everything hinged on her mood and whether she'd been able to get hold of food and medication.

Since Mamá was obsessed with the political situation, to cheer her up, I sent her an iPad through a friend. Given her arthritis, a tablet seemed more intuitive and straightforward than a computer. It kind of worked. She tried to learn English with Duolingo, played memory games, and consumed Twitter, Facebook, and YouTube content non-stop. Her passion for news felt futile, especially given the circumstances. But it was still a passion, which was critical for someone like her; she repeatedly told me, "I don't have a reason to live." Having to hear my mother go on about death was another form of torture—not unlike psychological terrorism. I didn't want to lose her, but there were times when I was convinced that I already had. Much as I tried to get her excited about things, what kind of future could I promise her when I couldn't even find solutions for her everyday problems?

Meanwhile, I tried to improve my relationship with Andrés. It was weird to picture him in uniform, policing the protests organized by the opposition—protests that the Chavistas referred to as "guarimbas"—when in the 1990s, with his hair long and a bandanna covering his face, he had taken pellet fire from that same police force. I would often see images of police brutality on the news. Everyone knew what went on in the police academy: corruption and abuses of power were to be expected, as were unofficial checkpoints and "matraqueos"—bribes offered in exchange for overlooking small things like traffic violations. I always wanted to believe that Andrés was different, that he had conviction. At the end of the day, he was my brother.

Andrés would tell me that being sent to break up protests was terrifying. He'd look up at the surrounding buildings, afraid of getting shot. He claimed he'd never physically injured anyone, and I wanted to believe him. Being a cop in Venezuela was neither easy nor well remunerated. Many officers diversified their work with "vaccination" schemes, which is how people referred to private security. A "vaccinated" establishment paid the police directly for additional surveillance. I doubt this concept was invented in my home country, though in Venezuela private security could be a matter of life or death. Andrés wasn't mixed up in any of that—at least that's what he told me—though several of his colleagues died during disagreements with their extracurricular clients.

We didn't like that Andrés was a police officer, not only because of their reputation but also because of the dangers involved. But Andrés insisted he was proud of his uniform and his responsibilities, which he felt he performed well. The way I saw it, he was running an unnecessary risk in a country where nothing was certain.

Mamá was worried about him, despite all the arguments and unhappiness. To her, he was the most vulnerable of her three children. At the same time, his aggressiveness and egotism made him difficult to talk to.

My conversations with Mamá became increasingly one sided. She had so many problems that I started limiting my responses to "I'm at work" and "Things are OK." I listened to her when she was sad, argued with her when she lost hope, and handled all the logistical minutiae that kept things running in her house.

Sometimes Mamá and I would talk about the past, though it was a delicate subject for her—her life now was caught between illness, insecurity, and the domestic dramas of everyday existence in Venezuela. To complicate matters more, she felt guilty about how my brothers had turned out. "I failed as a mother" was her tacit apology for having gotten an epidural when giving birth to Luis or letting the obstetrician use forceps on Andrés. "It's my fault. They hurt him during labor and goodness knows how it affected him," Mamá said of Andrés one day, as if she were getting the burden of motherhood off her chest for the first time. I learned from her that women are doomed to carry around feelings of sadness and guilt.

I came to the conclusion that Mamá would've been happier without children, though I never asked whether she'd wanted to be a mother. She always cited the cliché that life doesn't prepare you for this, that she hadn't learned how to be a mother from her mother, a woman she claimed to love deeply but rarely talked about, which I'd always taken as evidence of a distant relationship. "The worst stuff always falls on women," she'd say, instilling in me the idea that having children was a decision to be made consciously, once I could care for them financially, "without a man's help." Later she changed her mind and said she wanted me to give her more grandchildren—but only if they stayed close to her. "There's no point, you're too far anyway," she would say, ending the conversation.

Over the years, I heard her say so many times that children should be planned. I didn't give any thought to the possibility of becoming a mother. But then life decided for me. When I phoned Mamá to let her know I was sterile, she mourned the news as though the uterus were hers, making me feel even guiltier. It's one thing to decide you don't want children, and another to hear that you lack the ability to procreate. It was as if my body were defective, and at the same time as if I could not succeed in any part of my life—not as a daughter, or as a sister, or as a professional. I didn't feel like the best wife and would never have the chance to be a mother. I barely talked to anyone about it. It helped that Fabiano already had a son, who was living with us at the time—if our marriage ended, it would not be because of my sterility.

I tried to lighten my mom's load by telling her that she'd been an excellent mother, that she'd done her best with what she had—but she needed to try to understand Andrés if she wanted their relationship to improve. "Your brother hates me," my mother used to say after venting about his bad manners and constant yelling. The battle had mostly been lost, but as things continued to deteriorate, I hoped my brother would take off his resentment-tinted goggles and see Mamá for what she really was: sick, elderly, and needful. My mom found ever more reasons to complain every day. I had to constantly reassure her not only of my brother's love but also of mine. It wasn't enough that I called and wrote her every day, sent her food and money, added minutes to her phone, and paid off the credit cards we used between transfers. I wasn't there, and that was unforgivable.

Mamá and I could be cruel, and we knew how to pierce each other with verbal barbs that sometimes stuck, even after we'd apologized.

"I respected your decisions and asked you to come home because it's what my heart wanted, but you have no idea the hurt you've caused— because you're not a mother and never will be," she yelled at me one night.

"Shame you didn't manage to have me aborted," I shot back with all the sarcasm I could muster before slamming down the phone.

It took less than ten minutes for the regret to hit, but some things just couldn't be unsaid. She felt guilty about the attempted abortion, and I had crossed a line by using something she'd trusted me with against her. At the same time, she knew it wasn't my fault I couldn't have children.

To what extent was this emotional warfare a consequence of what we were living through? I couldn't say—all I knew was that I was exhausted, which I finally worked up the courage to tell her. In the heat of the moment, she admitted that she felt like a burden. It became obvious that we didn't have what it took to survive the collapse of Venezuela as a family.

My mother started going to the state-run market less and less; at the end of the day, there wasn't much point, and she got help from me. But not everyone was so lucky. Pensioners like my mother never got more than minimum wage, which was impossible to live on with the constant rise in prices. In 2016, the government announced four minimum wage hikes in an absurd attempt to correct stratospheric levels of inflation.

Even so, the minimum wage that year increased to just fifty-eight dollars a month on the parallel market.

But these wage hikes applied only to people in the workforce. Retirees made around seventeen dollars a month. In other words, one of the most vulnerable segments of the population—people over seventy—had no good access to health care or money for something as basic as food. Younger people, who got bonuses or worked for companies that paid more competitive salaries, not only had more money in their pockets but also could stand in line longer and do the daily dance of hopping from one market to the next to buy food.

There were additional challenges to shopping at the state-run markets: for example, a rotation system based on the last digit of people's identification numbers determined entry, so that they could only go to a particular market on a specific day of the week. If the members of a single household had identification numbers that ended in different digits, they were able to go to the same market on different days. On top of that, there were rules that either restricted how much of one food you could buy or forced you to purchase food in set packages. If you just needed milk, you might have to buy a set that also came with rice, beans, and sugar, which you would then barter or resell to your neighbors.

Naturally, these dashes to get food had an effect on the country's precarious infrastructure. Children missed school to stand in line at the supermarket, and adults didn't show up to work for the same reason. Everyone was standing in line for food.

The currency exchange control, which was supposed to be a temporary measure with the theoretical goal of protecting the country's reserves, lasted more than ten years and led to an endless string of illegal profit-making strategies. The bolívar depreciated year after year, until it was worth more as paper than as money.

Living in a country where inflation and devaluation were the norm and almost everything was imported meant existing in a permanent state of psychological terror; it meant accepting that it made no sense to work for minimum wage because it was impossible to get to the end of the month on the same amount of money that you'd managed to live on the month before.

Not only was minimum wage worthless, but it also wasn't possible to take your paycheck straight to the supermarket to do your shopping before the prices went up. The International Monetary Fund (IMF) reported that Venezuela had ended the past year with an inflation rate of over 400 percent. At that pace, the salary of the average Venezuelan began depreciating even before it reached the bank. No wage increase could change that.

Luz, who went home to La Guajira on Saturdays, started showing up for work later and later on Mondays, until finally she came on Tuesdays instead. She didn't have a cell phone, and the only way to reach her was at her sister's house via a landline that was rarely answered. She never let us know if she was running late, or if she wouldn't be coming at all. With no way to call her, my mother would wait for hours before concluding that Luz just wasn't going to show up. Luz would justify her tardiness by claiming the buses were few and far between. Other times, she'd say that she was sick, or that her mother was. I didn't want to waste time determining whether she was lying. She wasn't in an easy situation. When she didn't show up, Mamá would call me, sitting on the edge of her bed, and complain about needing to have her breakfast at the right time. Luz would prepare meals for my mother to heat up on the weekend, but Monday wasn't included because she was supposed to be back by then. When she didn't show up, the first order of business was to get the chores done; the second was to create a backup plan in case Luz never returned. But our only backup plan was to find someone to replace her, and the few people who were available for work either were untrustworthy or didn't pass muster with my mother. I didn't pressure Luz too much, in part because I was terrified of letting someone into the house who would then mistreat my mother. I was always picturing tragic scenarios. Every Monday morning when Luz didn't make an appearance, I'd have to improvise and ask a neighbor or my ex-sister-in-law for help. Simple as it may seem, finding someone to troubleshoot the situation and comfort my mother was a complex operation.

At the same time, I had other problems to deal with. My husband and I were supposed to go back to Brazil around mid-2016, when his scholarship ended. But I didn't have a job waiting for me there. I was so tired and scared to start from scratch again that when I received a job offer with my old company in Uruguay, I decided to go. It was one of the most difficult decisions I'd made. Unexpected situations were taking me farther and farther from the person I'd left everyone and everything behind for. I was starting to feel like I was losing my way, like things were out of control. I tried to convince myself that moving to Uruguay would bring me professional and financial stability that ultimately would take me back to São Paulo. But leaving Fabiano was one of my hardest goodbyes, and the following months would be even worse.

My mother disapproved of my decision and predicted that I would end up alone. "All you think about is work. There's more to life, honey. What I wouldn't give to have your father back," she wrote to me one day.

Work wasn't the only thing I thought about, but ever since leaving home, I'd lived in constant fear of being unable to support myself. Since I was twenty years old, I'd felt uprooted, and all I wanted at this point in life, after more than a decade of moving and starting over, was a fulfilling job and a stable home. I'd think back on my mother's words while I gazed out the window at the endless Uruguayan winter, feeling sad and cold as the wind howled outside. I kept tweaking my plans, even though I'd known since leaving Venezuela that there was no point in making them. I thought about my dad, who seemed incapable of saving money or plotting a future, and about my mother, who was obsessed with saving money for a future that never arrived. I was tired. That was it—I was tired of trying. I'd been living for two years with my suitcases always close at hand; I'd spent even longer trying to build a home first by myself, and then with my husband, and put down roots. But every time, something changed, or it wasn't enough. I didn't know it yet, but I would live in Uruguay for only seven months before moving back to São Paulo. At the time, all I could think about was the fact that I'd be living in a strange place on my own. "I won't end up alone, Mamá. I'm already alone," I once typed out in a message I never sent.

Mamá was obsessed with loneliness, and so was I. She talked more and more about Papá and how she missed him. It annoyed her to have to live with Luz. The only one of my mother's sisters who was still in Maracaibo didn't visit often, and when she did, she never stayed long. Only one of Mamá's neighbors dropped by to see her. Luis's former girlfriend Júlia lived three kilometers away with her teenage son, but they barely had time to visit. Júlia was pulling double shifts as a nurse at the university hospital to pad her income. She and Luis had separated a decade earlier, and even though she was working to be as independent as possible, she was finding it harder by the day to make ends meet, just like everyone else. Despite her grueling routine, whenever Mamá had a health emergency, Júlia was the first one on the scene.

My mother killed time with cable TV and movies she watched on her iPad via a shared Netflix account. If she was in a good mood and not in pain, she also cooked. In these moments of culinary inspiration, Mamá bemoaned the shortages of food and kitchenware. She would watch cooking shows on TV, wishing she could make the recipes herself. I bought her everything she asked for: a grill, an arepa maker, a blender, ceramic knives. I also sent her ingredients I didn't understand, like corn syrup, and her beloved pistachios to keep her in good spirits.

"Look, mamita, we made pan dulce for our afternoon snack," she wrote me in an email once, and attached a photo of golden, sugar-encrusted rolls that looked exactly like the ones she used to buy for us kids at La Concordia bakery in San Cristóbal.

She liked to sing along to music as well. Since she couldn't move her legs, she'd move her arms to the rhythm of the songs. "Mija, won't you give me your legs?" she'd ask me mischievously now and then. I'd laugh and say, "What do you mean, Mamá! You want me to end up in a wheelchair?" "Well, I'm the better dancer, you know," she'd joke.

In those brief moments of calm, we'd chat on FaceTime, which replaced Skype after she got her iPad. I'd send her pictures of Bubú, my poodle that she adored. My mother had become adept at navigating the virtual world. She was always sending me videos, texts, and voice messages by email, Facebook, and Twitter. And when she sent me pictures or emojis, I was truly happy. It felt like I had my mother back, and her silliness made me laugh. It was a relief not to talk about shortages or dollars.

Luis bought a phone for her and brought it back when he came home from Panama in late 2016. She mastered its basic functions in no time at all. The only thing Mamá couldn't master was her patience: she'd call me over and over again until I picked up. Mostly she called to ask how to download movies on Netflix or change her online banking password. She was happy to have Luis back, and since I was trying to improve things with Andrés, I started speaking more with Luis as well. In practice this meant that I went on about the fact that I didn't know what to do with my life while he listened in silence, giving no advice. My hope was that he'd spend more time with our mom, but it was in vain. He was only home for a few weeks, and then he left for Chile, where he was sure more opportunities awaited him.

Since Fabiano and I had lived in different countries all year, and with Venezuela's crisis worsening, I decided to spend Christmas and New Year's in Brazil with him. It was the first time I didn't go home for the holidays. I was hoping the trip would help us reconnect, but shortly after I arrived in Brazil, I realized that our relationship, which was already fractured, had been pulverized by old problems aggravated by distance. The request for a divorce arrived in early 2017, at the same time I learned that the news agency I worked for was transferring me to São Paulo as a correspondent. *Ironies of life,* I could hear my mom say. But she only spoke to me in my imagination; I didn't dare tell her anything. Through three months of daily phone calls, I kept silent. Whenever she asked me about Fabiano, I always answered, "He's fine, he sends his regards." I just didn't know how to tell her that we had separated. I worried that it would break her heart and she would judge me; at the end of the day, I felt like a failure. She had enough pain in Venezuela as it was—she didn't need more.

So I waited until I visited her in March and broke the news in person. The first thing I noticed after unloading my two large suitcases of food in the garage were stacks of empty Amazon boxes, which I'd been using to send groceries to her by ship. When I walked in, I sat in the living room, as always, to have coffee with her and chat. I asked her about the CLAP box in a corner of the kitchen. It was tiny compared to the boxes I sent her every two or three months.

"I took it for Luz. You know I don't even open the door when they knock, if it's for me," she responded, clearly irritated.

I'd never seen a CLAP before, except on the news. When I opened it, the contents seemed unbalanced, like they'd thrown in whatever they had on hand—as if these were the products of the season. There were several packets of spaghetti, but no rice or milk. I also saw beans, corn flour, a few bottles of mayonnaise, and one bottle of ketchup. Almost everything was imported, and the box was stamped with Chávez's face and signature.

There we were, talking about food boxes instead of my divorce. Somehow it was easier to talk about logistics than something so personal, but I finally got the news off my chest. Mamá fell silent and then asked me what had happened. I didn't know what to say. What hadn't happened? I'd spent years mechanically saying, "Everything is fine," so Mamá had no idea about anything. Since this didn't seem like the moment to change things, I didn't go into details. I just gave her a generic "Things didn't work out."

To distract her from the divorce, I brought up a topic I knew she'd love to weigh in on: my apartment. I told her that my tenant refused to pay or move out—she didn't even pick up when I called anymore. I didn't know what to do, or how to get that woman out of there. A friend had advised me to forget about it, no matter how frustrated I felt: "Pretend that the country doesn't exist. No more Caracas, no more apartment building." I hadn't seen the apartment since I bought it in 2010. Sometimes I got so worked up thinking about it that I would've paid whatever it took to recoup it. Other times, I could see that my friend's words made sense, and it all felt like it was happening to someone else. I didn't have savings, but I had a well-paying job, clothes, and some furniture and appliances, thanks to the work I'd done after leaving the country. I was in a better situation than when I left, with life experience I couldn't imagine having gotten if I'd stayed in Venezuela. Life had been kind to me. And that felt fine.

For what felt like the first time, my mother didn't pressure me on the issue and instead kept silent. In fact, Mamá was not only in good spirits for the duration of my stay but also the steady, supportive presence I'd been missing for so long. Maybe it was because of my divorce news. Whatever the reason, I was grateful for her motherly affection.

That visit home marked my transition between Uruguay and Brazil, where I would restart again—not from scratch, but alone. I was sad but also excited that after seven years of trying to find some direction with my career, I would finally have a steady job. And with a permanent contract, it was reassuring to know that I wouldn't have to move again anytime soon and that although this transition would be difficult, I would have time to adjust. Over the last decade I had relocated internationally five times and lived in a dozen places. The instability of freelancing had left me professionally insecure and full of anxieties. I was tired. My only constant had been Bubú, who had accumulated a file of travel permits and documents in four languages. I was ready to get an apartment, unpack my suitcases, and make it our home. I was ready to start again, once and for all.

Before leaving, I talked to Luz, and after conceding to yet another raise, I promised to find someone to work from Saturday to Monday, giving her one more day off. My promise was a bit like a campaign pledge: I had no idea how I'd make it happen. In any case, it bought me some time to come up with a solution. There was no way my mother could live in Chile with Luis or in Brazil with me—just making the trip would have been an odyssey for someone in her poor health, and we couldn't afford to pay someone to travel with her, or buy her health insurance outside of Venezuela, or rent an apartment that was accessible for someone who couldn't walk and had almost no muscular strength.

Andrés promised to check in on her but said Mamá didn't want him to move in with her. It was true. She had long complained that he didn't pay enough attention to her and was hardly any help. "I prefer being on my own," she said. I knew my brother, so I didn't press too much. Mamá once again refused to leave the house behind, and I left Venezuela feeling as uneasy as ever. It was clear that things were only getting worse, and that our arrangement with Luz could come to an end at any moment. I felt like a dog chasing its tail. Every solution was temporary and conditional, and I suffered in anticipation, imagining catastrophic scenarios.

Gone were the days when Chávez could fire up crowds on Caracas's Avenida Bolívar and promise the moon to the people of Venezuela. A storm had swept through and left the country in ruins in the futureless future that we were now living.

Yet in 2017, four years after Chávez's death, Maduro was still calling him "supreme leader," "beloved Comandante," and "eternal leader," fawning over him in public and using his name and image as if trying his hand at mind control or emotional manipulation—though it seemed to have the opposite effect. Some people still supported the government and bought into the explanation that international sanctions were the reason things were so cataclysmic. But even though the sanctions backed by some opposition leaders did exacerbate it, the damage was done long before Venezuela was penalized on the world stage. And many people who for years had defended Chavismo were now expressing their frustration with Maduro, whom they saw as responsible for the debacle. "This didn't happen with Chávez" became a popular expression. In an attempt to piggyback on his predecessor's formulas, Maduro kept launching welfare programs. That was how the "homeland card," a new form of national ID that gave people access to bonuses and government assistance, came into existence. My mother, who had stopped going to the state-run supermarkets, refused to sign up for one. The opposition criticized it, viewing it as a mechanism of surveillance and partisan division. But Mamá's refusal to sign up had more to do with pride. To her, signing up was as good as accepting "charity" from the government.

Luis, who had found a new job as a waiter in Santiago de Chile, talked a lot about the contrast he saw between the two countries. Unlike Venezuela, Chile had a stable economy, work opportunities, and conveniences for immigrants, or so he'd heard. Luis tried to persuade Andrés to go with him. After all, Andrés was always complaining about the fact that he didn't bring home enough money as a police officer to support his two small children, who lived with their respective mothers. But he wouldn't leave. He acknowledged the economic difficulties—there was no way to pretend the country wasn't falling into the grips of a ravenous hunger—but for him it was all a consequence of the international sanctions. Andrés's revolutionary nonsense knew no bounds. He lived in a working-class neighborhood in a modest house he'd built himself, drove a secondhand car, and was always lamenting that he didn't have this thing or that—all the while unable to admit that the government had its faults.

During the early years of the crisis, emigration was an option for middle-class people willing to invest all they had in airplane tickets and a new beginning. But the current desperation—in a country where things had taken on a permanent sheen of illegality and everything happened with tips, favors, bribes, or the help of money changers and smugglers—had led to never-before-seen images of thousands of Venezuelans crossing the border on foot, carrying nothing but what they could hold in their hands.

It's a difficult figure to pin down, but according to the United Nations, after several years of migration, 695,000 Venezuelans were living abroad by the end of 2015.[11] In the years that followed, the flow of migration ballooned, topping four million people in 2019, or 14 percent of the country's population.

Venezuela reached a point where there was no food or medication. Water, telephone, and internet infrastructure failed dramatically. Most international companies had closed their offices. Hospitals had succumbed to neglect and lack of supplies. Local money was good for nothing more than origami. People did not feel safe at home or in the streets. The police were corrupt; the justice system was inoperative. Protesting could lead to being shot, tortured, or forgotten in a dungeon. The schools and universities functioned poorly. Young people were leaving the country, leading to brain drain and a depleted workforce. Venezuela was now making international news because paper for documents was so scarce that it was impossible to issue a marriage or death certificate. Living was a daily endurance test, with the only reward being the possibility of opening your eyes the next day to face more challenges. It was too much to bear, even for the most fervent Chavistas

---

11 "Refugees and migrants from Venezuela top 4 million: UNHCR and ION," UN Refugee Agency, June 7, 2019, https://www.unhcr.org/en-us/news/press/2019/6/5cfa2a4a4/refugees-migrants-venezuela-top-4-million-unhcr-iom.html.

like my brother Andrés. As time whittled his police officer's salary down to $3.40 a month by the end of 2017, disillusion took deeper and deeper root inside him, until one day he just gave up.

"I'm leaving, I don't care how, there's nothing for me here."

He'd decided he would go to Chile because Luis was there, even though, practically speaking, Santiago was as abstract to him as, say, Tbilisi. But leaving wouldn't be easy.

Andrés couldn't afford a plane ticket. To get to Santiago, he would need to cross eight thousand kilometers through three countries. Desperate for money to finance the trip, he accepted an offer to sell his house for $5,000 USD, which had become the main currency in the streets, even though the government kept repeating that the real currency was bolívares. Though I didn't usually intervene in Andrés's affairs, I made a point of entering this argument. I couldn't believe someone could hand over a house for so little. "It makes sense for him to sell. If he leaves, the government is going to take it anyway as an expropriation. And if he rents it to someone, it'll be the same story with your apartment. At least he got a few dollars out of it. It's better than nothing," Mamá said. There was some truth to this.

A couple arrived at Mamá's house with $5,000 stuffed in an envelope. In return for their cash, they would receive the keys, the deed, and the signature on an improvised document that theoretically sealed the transfer of property. No records, no notaries, no bureaucracy. "None of that works here anymore," my brother shouted when I told him that he needed records and the whole thing looked like a scam. The thing is, the country had changed so much that I couldn't keep up. "You don't understand how things are here," Andrés told me.

To get to Chile, he would also need a passport. He'd never given much thought to traveling outside Venezuela, with the exception of a handful of trips to a border city in Colombia, which didn't require a passport; the trip to Cúcuta was practically a rite of passage for those of us born in the western part of the country. Getting a passport had never been a priority for Andrés—now it was an obsession.

But getting papers in Venezuela was another feat of epic proportions. For months Andrés visited the offices of ID services in various cities across the country, where he always got the same answer: "We don't have the materials." He reached out to friends, because in Venezuela it always takes a friend of a friend to make things happen. One time he was blackmailed, and another time he was scammed by the friend of a friend, who charged triple the document's official value and gave him nothing in return. According to accounts I've heard from acquaintances and friends, the average wait for a passport ranged from eight months to a year, though it wasn't an exact science. In addition to supply issues for the materials required to produce the booklets, the very same civil servants tasked with issuing them were conducting illegal passport sales in dollars to meet high demand, as citizens living abroad applied for identity documents and thousands upon thousands of people tried to leave the country.

People left however they could—by plane, by car, by bus, and even on foot. Images of pedestrians overwhelming the Simón Bolívar bridge that connects Venezuela to Colombia—the same bridge I'd crossed countless times to go shopping with my mother—went around the world. It made me emotional not just because I'd seen my country's collapse unfold in slow motion, but because I was one of the privileged. Maybe that's what spurred me to become more involved in Andrés's decision and help out as much as I could. I started learning about how other people had done the journey he wanted to do. There were tons of blogs by Venezuelans detailing their experiences and sharing tips on the safest routes for leaving the country. But what Andrés needed most of all was to be able to pay for expedited passport delivery online. It sounded easy, but nothing in Venezuela was easy. He had to keep clicking on a link until a payment form opened. My mother and I spent weeks taking turns helping him click. Nothing. We tried different browsers, connections, and times of day, especially early in the morning. Nothing.

Christmas rolled around, and my brother still hadn't gotten his passport. He and I had gotten closer, and things had relaxed between him and my mother, too. They even decided that he should move in with her temporarily in late 2017, to give Luz some vacation time. It was a last-minute decision, driven by the fact that we didn't have enough cash to give Luz for her weekly bus trips to La Guajira. How much we paid her didn't matter—without cash, there was no way for her to come and go.

Vital service disruptions were becoming more and more frequent, and the once-sporadic blackouts now happened without warning almost every day, making life especially hard in Maracaibo, one of the hottest cities in the country. As a result of the outages, internet and cell phone service was also unreliable, as were landlines.

Because of work, I couldn't travel home for the holidays that year. On Christmas Eve, I called my mother a few times, but she never picked up. Though my anxious mind jumped immediately to the worst-case scenario—faceless men looming over her, small and fragile in her red wheelchair—the increasingly frequent service interruptions meant a blackout was about as probable as a break-in.

We talked the following day, and Mamá said there'd been a power outage, right in the middle of Christmas. After dinner, Andrés went to visit his children. But she decided to stay home. She was scared of being mugged on the way back, in the deserted midnight streets of Maracaibo.

Right before the new year, Andrés called to say he was ready to go. He'd finally managed to pay for his passport, which would arrive at any moment. When he spoke to me with tears in his eyes and his voice choked with emotion, our sense of accomplishment was not unlike what Uruguayan striker Luis Suárez must've felt when he shot the ball into England's net during the 2014 World Cup, one month after getting an arthroscopy. Against all odds, he had come back to life.

Mamá didn't immediately react to the news from her last child still in Venezuela, and instead focused on current events. Headlines such as "The Pernil Revolution," "Venezuelans Ask for Food on Christmas," and "At Least 22 Detained for Christmas Eve Looting in South" were flooding social media. Even though the money we sent made it possible for her to pay for food no matter the price, there was no normalizing the situation. Before Christmas, two chickens had cost 600,000 bolívares, she said—but just days later, the same two chickens now cost 700,000.

We had the same conversation every day, though the subject sometimes expanded to include eggs, bread, rice, milk. I couldn't get my mother to understand the meaning of "inflation," at least not inflation that closed out 2017 at 2,000 percent and that the IMF projected would reach 13,000 percent in 2018. It was hard for her to understand that her teacher's pension, which had once gotten her a house, was no longer enough for two chickens. My mother, who used to brag about her financial strategies for raising a family as a widow, could not unlearn how to be frugal. She couldn't deal with the fact that she had to spend her money the second it arrived, because leaving it in the bank was as good as setting it on fire. That wasn't in her nature; she couldn't help it. When she got a transfer, she always saved a part of it because it made her anxious—truly anxious—to leave her bank account empty. She lied to me about it so she could hold on to the safety of having numbers in her bankbook. It took a biblical effort on my part to convince her to use my credit card and hers to stay a step ahead of inflation. "I don't want to get into debt," she said.

The rampant devaluation confused her even more. I could have blamed her age—she was seventy-two—but the truth is that the illogical math would have confused anyone. Even though she knew the bolívar was worthless, she got lost in calculations that required ever more zeros. In 2010, shortly after I left the country, a dollar cost 8 bolívares. Seven years later, in June 2017, it cost 7,780 bolívares. In December of the same year, a dollar cost more than 100,000 bolívares. The escalation was so dizzying that the next year, in 2018, the government knocked five zeros off the currency; even so, it wasn't long before the exchange rate added another five. Under these conditions, those with relatives outside the country had an advantage over those who didn't: they could eat.

On New Year's Eve, Luis called me from Chile. We'd exchanged a few messages in the last few months, after he finally downloaded WhatsApp. He always greeted me with "¡Hola, mami!"—that Caribbean custom of calling people "mami" or "papi" no matter your family ties. Still, our conversations were spare, and nearly always revolved around how much money we needed to send Mamá. She'd told me Luis shared an apartment with a group of Venezuelans to save money; he'd been assigned the sofa. He walked an hour to and from work to save on transit. Even so, Luis was always enthusiastic about everything. He'd be turning forty-two soon, but he was the same man I'd known twenty years earlier: eager, spontaneous, incapable of sitting still. Tireless and strangely optimistic, he was determined to follow the rainbow to its pot of gold.

We talked about personal issues, and it became clear that despite the affective and geographic distance between us, his little sister could still make him emotional. Now that it looked like I was getting my family back, nostalgia tightened its grip even more. In the past few months, my brothers seemed to have come to understand that when you migrate, any advantages are financial, never emotional. And that even though I was in a better situation, with a white-collar job and a good salary, we all suffered and felt lonely; none of us could go home. I had learned that the migration stories that most upset me were my own brothers'. We discussed Andrés's imminent journey, and Luis said he'd be happy to take our brother in, but given the uncertainty of his own situation, Andrés would have to hit the ground running.

We wished each other a happy new year without, I think, giving too much thought to our hopes for the next twelve months. Trying to make plans felt like a pointless exercise. I didn't eat any grapes that night. I didn't make any wishes. Alone in my apartment in São Paulo, I was just grateful to see another January 1, and I was determined not to cry. Things may not have been going according to plan, but at least they were going.

In Maracaibo, my mother was annoyed because the power had gone out again. When it came back, the internet stopped working. The landline was down too. We found out service was cut due to outstanding payments, as the fees had increased tenfold overnight. When Mamá and I finally talked, she told me she was feeling cheery because her sister had brought over a bunch of bananas.

"I haven't had bananas for weeks. I got them from Eva, who went downtown."

"You've already gone to the supermarket, right?" I asked.

"I went, but they didn't have anything. There's nothing in stock during the week. They sell what little they get to their employees or to the communal councils that are enrolled."

"Are you part of a communal council?" I asked tentatively, because I knew my mother hadn't wanted to sign up for a government program, much less participate in one of the neighborhood associations Chávez had instated years earlier—just another grassroots initiative designed to redistribute administrative power and uphold his national project.

"I am, but the markets aren't accepting any more councils right now, so mine couldn't buy anything. The guard said things are arriving on Sunday for sale to the public, and I should get there early."

Following the guard's advice, Mamá and Andrés got to the supermarket Sunday at 7:30 a.m. There was already a line; apparently, she wasn't the only one who'd been tipped off. That afternoon, she told me about the adventure in a video call.

"They were going to let the elderly in first, but when the doors opened, everyone went in. I was scared. I thought I would get my legs broken."

"They let everyone in at the same time?"

"There's no order, mija, everyone wants food. There were no soldiers there. How were they supposed to do it?"

"Well, did you get anything?"

"Yes," she said, smiling like a mischievous child. "Two kilos of flour, a tube of toothpaste, and butter."

A few days later, his departure imminent, Andrés went to Caracas with his ex-wife and one of his children to validate some personal documents. By land, the trip was almost seven hundred kilometers—the same route I used to travel every three or four months when I lived in Caracas and went home to visit Mamá, or that we'd traveled together when she came to stay with me. Back then, the journey was what a friend described as an adventure combining scenes straight out of *Mad Max* with obstacles worthy of Indiana Jones. The arteries connecting different points in northern Venezuela run parallel to the revered Caribbean coast, which stretches for nearly three thousand kilometers. My family had covered many of those kilometers during the trips Papá would take us on. Decades later, those same highways—now abandoned and in continuous decline—had turned into hot spots for robbery and murder.

On the way to Caracas, Andrés spent a couple of days in Tucacas, a small seaside resort surrounded by crystalline waters and several capital cities, which made it a popular holiday destination. He sent me photos of my three-year-old nephew splashing in the Caribbean for the first time, interspersed with reflections on the contrasts of this new Venezuela: malnourished children in an impoverished town that served tourists who "threw money into the air" at the town's resorts.

That same night, less than two hundred kilometers from Tucacas, coastal poverty took on a new dimension. At least four Venezuelans died and dozens went missing after their boat sank on the way to Curaçao. The news reverberated, highlighting a new facet of the despair: hundreds of Venezuelans launching themselves into the sea on perilous crossings, seeking a better life on neighboring islands.

With Andrés on the road and no cash to pay Luz, we finally found someone to help my mother for a few days. Amparo lived far away and couldn't stay overnight, but she committed to arriving before 9:00 a.m. while my brother was gone. Still, with public transit on its own irregular schedule, it was impossible to fix a time beyond "I'll try to get there."

The nation's bus fleet was shrinking, affected not only by the lack of spare parts and new vehicles but also by the fact that there was almost no cash in circulation. As a result, public transportation had been reduced to chance appearances by junk vehicles stuffed with people. These poorly maintained buses, so rusty that I was afraid to touch them—"If you cut yourself, you'll get tetanus"—had been common in the Maracaibo of my childhood. Their arbitrary stops were often preceded by someone shouting, "After the light!" or "At the corner!" As soon as the bus came to a stop, the fare collector would be dangling out the door, getting off and on with circus-like agility. Inspired by the Héctor Lavoe salsa song, the collector would say, "Come in, I can fit a hundred," while shoving in new passengers who squeezed in where they could. The other option was a por puesto car: some operated on fixed routes, while others functioned as "pirate" cars. In my teenage years, Maracaibo went through a public transit evolution. Some of the bus lines were formalized, with new vehicles and defined stops. Waiting for the bus at a specific spot instead of a random street corner felt like the height of modernity. At first it was hard to remember to push a button instead of shouting, "At the corner!" The expansion of bus routes had led to a decrease in "chirrincheras," pickup trucks that people piled into like sacks of cement, often on routes that terminated in La Guajira. But now, in 2018, chirrincheras were the main form of public transportation. They'd pack in as many people as possible, and the passengers would hold themselves up however they could, sometimes with the pressure of other people's bodies, as the pickups traveled through the city beneath the dogged sun, charging fares at their discretion.

That was something my mother didn't have to deal with. We'd managed to keep her in a bubble, up to a point—but she was affected by the consequences of the collapsed public transportation system. Just as we struggled to find someone to be her aide, it was an uphill battle to find someone to paint the walls, waterproof the roof, or do any maintenance around the house. With Andrés leaving for Chile, and relations between my brothers and me on the up-and-up, I broached the possibility of selling the house and using the money to pay for a couple of months in a nursing home in Santiago; we might be able to cover the fees between the three of us. It could be a temporary fix: Mamá would have access to health care and two of her children, and it'd be faster and cheaper for me to travel to Chile than to Venezuela. For the first time, she gave the idea some consideration. The real estate agent she called did an eyeball appraisal and made an offer: the two-hundred-square-meter house she'd been refusing to leave for years could sell for $8,000. A week later, that figure fell to $6,000. As if it already weren't obvious, the agent felt obligated to say, "Things are complicated."

Mamá responded firmly that she would not sell the house. I didn't push back, so the plan was ruled out.

The year 2018 had started with a bang. Rumors of a military revolt, which made the rounds every so often, reached Chile. Mamá told me she'd nervously gone out to buy things at Luis's insistence. He'd called and told her there was talk of rebellion and deposited money for her to stock up while she could. It was reasonable to believe in this kind of rumor in an always-tense country, especially in times when soldiers were also struggling to make ends meet. A Reuters photo depicting two soldiers apparently searching for goods in garbage bags shocked the country during those days. If the soldiers were in such need, why should they remain loyal to the government?

For my brother, the rumors made sense. "The people don't want to go out into the street anymore," Andrés said. "No one wants to see their children get killed—how many people do you think died during the protests? All that's left is the military, because now their pockets are getting hit, now their economic interests are being affected. Their salaries can go up as much as they want—but what are they going to do with millions of bolívares?"

But in Venezuela, the military had taken advantage of what little power they had, first with help from Chávez and then from Maduro, dismantling loyalties and founding a dynasty in which thousands of generals had rank and power but no troops. All the same, Caracas did experience a couple moments of tension that January, when there was an avalanche of news about a confrontation on the outskirts of the city. Officials had cornered Óscar Pérez, an ex–police officer who'd skyrocketed to fame the year before for stealing a helicopter and calling for an insurrection.

During the shoot-out, a visibly scared Pérez shared a couple of short videos on social media saying he wanted to surrender but they were firing into the house where he was staying. His death was confirmed by authorities. "Mission complete," Maduro proclaimed hours later.

My mother, who was in a worse mood than usual when we spoke later, said that she—a nonpracticing Catholic—had even fought with God. "There are people here dying of hunger and illness—where is the divine justice? We're dying," she shouted into the phone.

"This morning I went to the supermarket. Nothing but flies. The employees told me there's no food, even for them—the government takes everything for their missions. There aren't even cashiers anymore." Her spirits were not lifted by the return of Luz, who was able to come back once my mother managed to get hold of a bit of cash.

Cash had become another obsession. On payday, the banks opened just for pensioners, but they only distributed money until they ran out of bills. The tellers at the government banks, where my mother got her money, limited individual withdrawals to 10,000 bolívares a day (0.0014 percent of her monthly pension), but that was also until they ran out of cash. There were always lines, and you could never be certain you'd be able to withdraw anything. In Venezuela, where there were shortages of everything, there was even an underground market for hard cash. But it wasn't easy for anyone. There was a two-way stream on the border with Colombia: products purchased in Venezuela at government-subsidized prices went to Maicao to be resold for several times their original price. In the other direction, key food items in short supply came into Maracaibo and were then sold at black markets in the center of the city.

These underground markets in downtown Maracaibo would also collect large quantities of cash that were then sold for commissions as high as 140 percent. "In December, I wondered how people could be stupid enough to pay two million bolívares just to get back a single bolívar note, but things have been so tough that last week I was more than happy to pay 100 percent commission for some cash," Andrés told me as he was about to leave, beaten down by a system that "takes advantage of our misery and makes us pay for everything, once, twice, a hundred times over."

The power cuts started to take their toll. My mother had lost five appliances in the span of a year, the last of them her air conditioner—an essential amenity in a city where temperatures top 85 degrees Fahrenheit all year round. The indiscriminate outages hit Maracaibo harder than anywhere else. My mother's house, a concrete bunker, was unbearable without air-conditioning. In just five minutes, the feeling of suffocation would get to be too much. My mother said it made her not want to eat. Unable to sleep in the oppressive heat, she'd wheel herself to the front of the house so she could breathe. At night, when everything had to be locked up, her despair felt more pressing. I started thinking about buying a generator. I talked about it with Luis, who immediately brought up two obstacles I had no way of addressing: who would turn it on when Luz wasn't there, and, if it ran on gas, how would they find a steady supply of fuel, which was also becoming scarce.

I listened to my mom and tried to console her, but I had no idea how to respond. I circled around the problems but failed to come up with a solution. When I did think of one, like the generator, I came up against a wall of more problems.

My fourteen-year-old nephew, the youngest of Luis's children, spent some afternoons with Mamá, while Júlia, his mother, worked double shifts at the hospital to earn extra money, even though it evaporated in seconds. My nephew was never much of a reader. When he was a child, I bought him books that he accepted politely but without enthusiasm. During high school, when he should've been preparing for college, he had to stop going to class. His school closed because the last of its teachers had left the country. The interruption not only set him back but also affected Júlia's ability to work. "I never thought we'd get to this point," my mother said. Luis had started talking to her about bringing my nephew to Chile.

I wrote and asked him not to tell his son about his idea, because Júlia would never condone it. "I don't like that the kid's having such a hard time. If it's up to me, he'll come live here," he responded in a voice message. Not wanting to make trouble, I asked him to try to have some empathy for his ex-wife. "Don't pit him against his mother," I said, trying not to overstep so we could avoid a fight.

Luis didn't talk with his two older kids. Carmen, his oldest, had recently moved to Falcón, a state four hours by car from Maracaibo. My parents used to take us there on vacation when we were children. The modest rental they'd get didn't have a TV or a radio, so my parents would wake us up early for breakfast, then sweep us off to the beach. Papá would set out an umbrella and chairs, Mamá a cooler full of sandwiches and water. We'd spend the whole day there and only leave in the evening. Back in the rental, Mamá made us shower right away, "no ifs, ands, or buts." Afterward, Andrés and I would walk with Papá through the streets of Adícora, the little coastal town where we always stayed. Papá would tell us stories about abandoned houses, lighthouses, and other oceans, while I chased the crabs that mocked me by scuttling into the endless holes in the ground. I'm romanticizing the past again, but there really was nothing better than those days full of salt and bread with Cheez Whiz.

Pedro, Carmen's younger brother, lived in Carabobo with his mother. Shortly after separating from Luis, Pedro's mother got married and added another girl to the family. Both Carmen and Pedro went to college and chose majors that now felt surreal. My niece, charmed by the famous collage of Venezuelan landscapes, majored in tourism. Her brother, who'd been fascinated by the diversity of birds in the country since he was a child, wanted to be an ornithologist. Though I encouraged them, I couldn't help but wonder if there was a future for them, for the vistas and the birds, and if they'd have any opportunities in the country my father had known as a "land of possibility." They ended up leaving Venezuela as well.

Andrés was on the cusp of emigrating, leaving his two kids behind. Though I felt that his move was bringing us a little closer emotionally, it was also true that, as José Alfredo Jiménez once sang, "Distances separate cities; cities destroy traditions."

Chapter 12

Tiny Catastrophes

I don't know how many times I've read and talked about hunger, shortages, and migrants in the past few years, or how these words came to replace "beauty queen" as Venezuela's calling card. But in 2018, what haunted me was my incapacity to find the words to convey the knot in my stomach every time I was confronted by a new challenge from afar, trying to maintain the basic living conditions my mom deserved and needed now that she was over seventy years old. The collapse of Venezuela was a swarm of daily tiny catastrophes.

Just as Andrés was getting ready to leave, my mother called to tell me that Luz was once again talking about resigning. In Los Filúos, the town where her family lived twenty kilometers from the border, the Colombian peso had become the de facto currency. Like thousands of other residents of La Guajira, her family regularly crossed into Colombia to buy things and sell livestock, their primary source of income. Their house didn't have electricity or running water. In those days, with the help of government subsidies, it cost $0.001 at the parallel exchange rate to fill a forty-liter gas tank with the highest octane. And that was after the 2016 price increase, the first in two decades. Luz's sister, also a domestic worker in Maracaibo, was moving to Colombia to work as a live-in for a family. They were both sick of the hundred-kilometer commute to Maracaibo; it could take as long as four hours because of the five checkpoints buses were forced to stop at in that land of oblivion. In those days, a ticket sold for 60,000 bolívares. We covered the cost of the trip in addition to her salary, but everything was transferred virtually. To get enough cash for a month's worth of bus tickets, Luz would have had to go to the ATM forty-eight days in a row—and that's assuming she could successfully withdraw cash every day and the ATM was close enough that she didn't have to spend money on transportation. That was never the case. "She's tired," Mamá told me. "Who cares if we keep raising her wages if I can't get her cash? She said if things stay this way, she's leaving. She's tired, and she has a point."

Andrés said that letting Mamá go to the center of the city to buy cash was out of the question. "The cash markets are run by mafias," he explained when I asked for advice. He'd only gone once, with a police contact. "This is a lawless place. I still have my convictions, but anyone with half a brain is getting out of here. I should've gone when Luis told me to—now I have to go alone, over land." There was such deep sorrow in his voice.

Not long after that, as I was chatting with Mamá on FaceTime one night, Andrés appeared on the screen out of nowhere and said, "I'm leaving." At the last minute, he'd decided to move his trip up by two days; Luis had called to say that the borders were closing and he needed to leave as soon as possible. While he devoured a sandwich, I watched him say goodbye to my mother, who looked stunned. The situation was so absurd and it all happened so fast, it was hard to feel anything. But he was leaving.

"I'll write as soon as I can. Wish me luck." He smiled, kissed Mamá, and left. Not even two minutes. I have to admit that until that moment, I was convinced something would happen to make him stay. It was just so hard to imagine Andrés outside of Venezuela; he had been so loyal to Chavismo, until he hit his breaking point.

"Make sure you give your brother a hand," my mother said dejectedly, gazing down at the floor. To cheer her up, I reminded her that I was going to be visiting on her birthday, in August, something I hadn't done since leaving Venezuela. But she told me she was afraid for me to come. "You don't know how it is here, mija," she said.

That same night, Andrés took a bus to San Cristóbal, where Mamá had grown up. From there, he'd continue to San Antonio, a city on the Colombian border. The day after he left, my worried mother called to say she hadn't been able to reach him, and could I try to get in touch.

Much to her relief, I managed to talk to Andrés not long after. He'd gotten to San Antonio that morning, but there were so many people crossing the border that getting stamped to leave Venezuela took a whole day, and entering Colombia took another day. He found a company selling one-way bus tickets to Santiago for $366 due to growing demand, but he'd arrived on a Saturday. He would have to wait until the ticket office opened again on Monday.

"It's horrible here. It's an exodus," he told me in a voice message. "We're not talking about immigration anymore—this is an exodus. Everything is a business. At the San Cristóbal bus terminal, there's a sub-terminal that deals in immigrant departures. As soon as you get off the bus you hear, 'Peru,' 'Chile,' 'Ecuador,' but the name you hear most often is 'San Antonio'—border city, mandatory stop. That short forty-minute trip costs 100,000 bolívares. All the money the taxi drivers earn in cash, they sell for double the value. Even the air is for sale here, no one has any scruples. It's sad. How much further can this country fall?"

Andrés sent me voice messages nonstop from the modest San Antonio hotel where he was staying until Monday. He sounded progressively more broken down.

"This is awful. I'm getting messages: they're saying the borders are closing, that no one will be able to cross, the guerrillas are here. I'm going to the Simón Bolívar bridge and I'll let you know."

A couple of hours later, he told me that the National Guard said he could leave on Monday if he got stamped, that it was business as usual, because the new normal at the border was this: thousands and thousands of people waiting in line and leaving one after the other, carrying with them only uncertainty and a few changes of clothes. As his departure time drew near, Andrés sent me message after message. I didn't even have a chance to respond, there were so many to listen to.

"This is horrible. I'm scared they're going to do something to send me back, but I can't, I'm almost on the bus. This is hell, this is utter carnage," he said. All I could do was tell him to have a little patience.

After crossing the bridge and touching Colombian soil, he told me he was getting on the bus, then left me one final voice message.

"This isn't the country you left. We've reached a breaking point. I knew it was going to be hard, but never this hard. Even though we have the best beaches in the world, the Auyán-tepui, Mount Roraima, and those birds our nephew likes so much, we have no choice but to leave. There's no future here. I'm not coming back. This country is bleeding out at the border."

Shortly after he left the country, I traveled to the Brazil-Venezuela border, where I saw for myself what Andrés had lived through. It was true: Venezuela was bleeding out.

In 2018, when Chávez's "revolution" celebrated its nineteenth anniversary, most of the people surrendering on foot to the country's borders, hauling as much weight as they could carry on their backs, were the same poor men and women he'd sworn to protect. That year, I took three trips to the Brazil-Venezuela border to cover the news. The first trip was devastating. The refugee shelters set up in Boa Vista, the capital of Roraima, in northern Brazil, were ramshackle and unhygienic. People slept on sidewalks and in public squares, and hung around doing nothing for days. I thought of my father when I saw this destitution, and of the fact that Venezuela, the country that had welcomed him after the war, was now hemorrhaging people, many of them disoriented and in tatters. People couldn't help but cry when they arrived in that small Brazilian city, chasing rumors of food and work, only to be met with a completely different reality. There were people who wanted to go home but couldn't afford fifteen dollars for the trip back to the border. So they stayed, like lost souls, waiting for something to happen.

Those days, most Venezuelans in Boa Vista camped out in the city's central square, which ironically was named after our national hero. Volunteers brought food now and then to Praça Simón Bolívar to alleviate the migrants' hunger. One afternoon, as I watched children and grown-ups lining up for hot dogs and water, my father's words popped into my head: "One day, when you don't have enough to eat, you'll remember this." This is how you lose everything from one day to the next, I realized.

I regretted not asking Papá more about his past, not doing enough research. I didn't know much about him at all. He was born in a village in the south of Spain. He had six siblings. His father, a man I was never able to call "abuelo" because he died four decades before I was born, had worked on a farm. Papá wasn't in school for long and claimed not to be afraid of the dead. He told me that as kids, he and his friend used to dare each other to walk through the cemetery at night. "It's the living you have to be scared of, mija," he said. I thought of this story whenever I went to the cemetery where he was buried, on the east side of Maracaibo. The cemetery was now abandoned, vandalized constantly, and lonelier by the day. Nervous about being robbed or jumped, I hadn't visited his grave in years. The headstone was plain, labeled only with his name and the dates of his birth and death, which his daughter from his first marriage had written in after his burial. Whenever I read news articles about the plundered graves in that cemetery, I was sorry that the helpless dead couldn't come back to life to scare off the people who defied the church's instruction to let them rest in peace. It made me sad to think someone could have opened the wooden box containing my father, who was buried wearing a borrowed white shirt, brown pants, and black shoes.

When I was little, I found it weird that Mamá had such a large family when Papá had only his kids and two nephews. He also talked about a sister who'd visited him a couple of times in Venezuela, but I never met her. He wasn't very attached to the past, and I don't know whether that was a personal choice or whether it had to do with the fact that in the Caribbean we lived in an eternal present. He told us a few stories, though, and I know he spent several years trying to reconnect with his brother through the Red Cross.

Before the advent of the internet, my father wrote letters and mailed them to Spain. He wrote first drafts of those letters in a notebook filled with his cursive handwriting. In them, he mentioned friends whose names I didn't recognize and alluded to things and places that were mere abstractions to me. When I saw Venezuelan migrants sleeping in the crowded, filthy tents of Boa Vista's earliest refugee shelters, I tried to picture Papá's first port of arrival, Puerto Cabello, where he quarantined before starting a new life in the tropical land tucked behind the mountains that separated the rest of the country from the Caribbean coast.

I don't know if Papá didn't make much of an effort to stay in touch with the rest of his family, or if their estrangement was simply the consequence of a time when letters took weeks to travel between continents and few people could afford international calls. I also don't know how it made him feel, not having a family to call his own. Papá said he took only a few letters and photos with him when he left Spain as a teenager during the civil war, and then he lost everything in some confrontation shortly before being captured in 1939. At home we had two old photos of him, and one of his mother, María Martínez. Of course, I never met my grandma either. Thanks to that photo, I know she had the same sad eyes as my father and Andrés. But it was the only physical trait Papá shared with his mother. He never told me anything about her, except that she'd died far away from him. "I never saw her again," he said to me one Sunday afternoon as he tearily showed me a photo with scalloped edges.

Papá had strong arms. He used to sit me on his knees and have me box with him by punching the palms of his hands. He taught me to love boxing movies. I remember our conversations in detail, which is strange given that I was just a kid. He called me his Caribbean pearl, something my brothers made fun of me for. Aside from that, I don't remember him using any other lovey-dovey terms. An acquaintance of his recently told me that my father always talked about how sweet I was. I thought he was sweet too, though his temper was undeniable: one time, I saw him beat up a guy who, for whatever reason, decided a hospital waiting room was a safe space for him to praise the Germans.

My father never forgot the war. I guess that's something you can't forget. At the same time, he kept his distance from it. I never saw him reach out to other veterans or express interest in visiting the Mauthausen concentration camp, which was still giving him nightmares four decades later. I read somewhere that the Mauthausen quarries were where the German soldiers tried to break the spirits of their Spanish prisoners. I've read several eyewitness accounts of what happened there. The torture those prisoners suffered would've been enough to destroy any person's soul. But not Papá's. The soul of the man who fought the Nazis, survived a concentration camp, then moved to Venezuela and helped conspire against the dictatorship there was never broken. Though we didn't have much time together, I worshiped him, and I did my best to keep even my smallest memories of him alive. Those memories were rekindled when I visited the United Nations High Commissioner for Refugees' shelters in Roraima, which were crowded with Venezuelans who'd turned into refugees without ever having known war.

Most of the people I interviewed on the streets of Boa Vista and Pacaraima on the Brazilian border had brought little more than a backpack or two packed with documents, a few changes of clothes, and reminders of the children, parents, siblings, or partners they'd left behind. They didn't have enough money to eat, much less to call their loved ones. Some had sold their phones to pay for their trip to Brazil. Conversations with their families in Venezuela were few and far between: some people hadn't talked to their relatives in months; others left them Facebook messages whenever they had five or ten reais to pay for a few minutes online. Many of them were younger than me. Most, if not all, came from eastern Venezuela. On that trip, I met only one person from Maracaibo.

José was twenty-one years old and a decent cook. He'd left his mother in Maracaibo with the promise of help, then set off for Caracas in search of work and money to send home. But the crisis was closing in and he didn't know anyone in the capital, so he moved on to the small coastal city of Puerto La Cruz, hoping to find a restaurant job or profit from the remnants of tourism. José came away empty handed, so he heeded the voices that spoke of a promising Brazil and saved up enough money to get to the border, which is where we met. He lived with other Venezuelans beneath a stage that had been built next to the posts marking the boundary between the two countries. They'd put up walls made of cardboard and trash bags to keep warm at night, but also to ensure a modicum of privacy. It'd been two weeks since José last spoke to his mother, who lived with his younger siblings in a low-er-middle-class neighborhood not far from Mamá's house. In the same way he'd managed to get to the border—little by little—he was saving up money to take him farther into Brazil, until he found someplace with work. We parted ways around noon, as he and his neighbors were preparing their first—and possibly only—meal of the day: black beans boiling on a small cooker fashioned out of a wheel. Suddenly, that scene struck me as a micro-portrait of what Venezuela had become—the set-ting of millions of tragedies.

José was just a baby in December 1998, when Chávez wrapped up his campaign promising to do whatever it took to redeem the dig-nity and morale of a depressed, beaten-down country. Four days later,

Chávez won the election. At the time, José lived in a cement house where he had a room of his own and lower-middle-class amenities. Now he was leading an itinerant life with whatever he could fit in his backpack, living in a place with no bathroom or infrastructure except plastic-and-cardboard walls and a concrete ceiling that was really a floor. His few items of clothing were drying on a makeshift clothesline strung between two boundary posts, symbols that announce the beginning of a country and that are romanticized every so often by leaders gesturing to our national sovereignty.

Sixteen years earlier, when I was José's age, I'd also traveled along the nearly two thousand kilometers that separate Maracaibo from Pacaraima. My trip took place in 2001, during a break in my junior year of college—prompted in part by my father's voice, which continued to echo in my head, insisting that it was important to get to know my country. I packed a small backpack with clothes, a tent, and dozens of materials and tools for crafting, and the cords that I used for juggling, and then a friend and I went from buses to public squares to cheap hotels. It took us more than a week to reach the border, but we weren't in a rush. Santa Elena de Uairén, on the Venezuelan side, was a small, peaceful village nestled in a unique landscape. Pacaraima, by comparison, looked like a sea of commercial warehouses. Back then, there weren't long lines of people waiting to cross the border. Truth be told, there was almost no one there at all. The region was mostly frequented by tourists on their way to Mount Roraima, which is said to have inspired Arthur Conan Doyle's mythical lost world. Now this remote location looked transformed by the abundance of people migrating in search of something better. Looking around, I felt fortunate for the life I had managed to build away from home and for being able to help my mom. But I also wondered how much further the country was going to fall. How much more would people have to suffer?

In those early months of 2018, it was impossible to get hold of hard cash in Maracaibo. What little Mamá received from her pension immediately went to Luz, who used it to pay her bus fare, while I covered the rest with daily transfers, since Mamá still found it hard to navigate online banking. When people began using screenshots of transfers as proof of payment, part of my day was taken up with sending screenshots to strangers who'd done something or other for her. People could also use debit and credit cards, but power cuts made them less and less functional.

Around that time, I decided to try to get back my Caracas apartment, which was still occupied by a tenant who hadn't paid rent in years. One time, when she was gone for a few weeks, the condo board emailed an address they'd found in the archives, not knowing who to contact about urgent repairs; the address happened to be mine. Because she'd signed into all the board meetings under my name, pretending to be the owner of my small apartment—or so I heard from the condo representatives when I called to explain my situation—they'd assumed they were writing to the woman they'd seen living in the building all those years. Thanks to a friend and the support of the board president, I managed to change the locks on the apartment, hoping to give an ultimatum to my tenant, who would have to show up sooner or later since all her belongings were there. It wasn't long before she came back and filed a report against me with the government's housing authorities, giving who knows what reason.

After endless phone calls and favors, I tracked down an employee at the office she'd gone to, and started pressuring them, too. I'd never known how to stand up for myself in that situation, yet I was doing it just like my mother had taught me to: with determination. I explained everything that had happened with the tenant from the beginning. I said that she refused to pay rent, and I acknowledged that yes, I had left the country and it was not my primary residence, but that did not mean I deserved to be robbed. Surprisingly, the housing authority employee took my side. The pressure worked. A week later, the woman left with all her things, though not before pulling out all the wiring in the apartment and vandalizing the bathroom, the kitchen, and the exterior plumbing. Finally, she filled the locks with superglue, forcing me to change them one more time. "At least she didn't pour cement down your drain," said the friend who'd helped me in Caracas. She was right—the woman could've done far worse than simply gut my apartment.

In Chile, Andrés and Luis were sharing a room, and finding it harder and harder to overcome their differences. Andrés wouldn't stop complaining to me about our older brother, who in turn said almost nothing about the strain between the two of them. They were polar opposites. While Luis did his best to make things work, Andrés had something to say about everything and everyone. In a long series of voice messages, he ranted about low salaries, xenophobia, and jobs that didn't meet his expectations. Convinced I was living well, he asked me for money I refused to give him because I didn't have any. He talked nonstop about Luis, and time and again said that we, his family, had never helped him.

"I talked to him all day. I don't know, sometimes I get this feeling, this sense that something's wrong. I don't think he was ready to leave Venezuela, but he did and now he's learning how to get by," my mother wrote to me in an email. "He's a grown-up but I don't want him to be in pain. He's still my kid. His pain is my pain." I sent back a string of sad emojis. I didn't know what to say. I tried to give Andrés advice, but I knew that if he insisted on holding on to his resentment, things would never change. I suggested he stop complaining about Luis and move out if he didn't like living with him, but Andrés clearly expected Luis to behave a certain way. He went on his usual diatribes against the family, telling stories about people I didn't know as proof that we'd failed him. I always said the same thing, that he had to focus on finding and holding a job, and then everything would gradually fall into place. But the closeness we'd managed to achieve months earlier was slowly dissipating. In her emails, my mother toggled between feeling sorry for him and being disappointed that "Andrés never learned how to live."

Andrés's tales of woe were still playing in the background when another problem cropped up: Luz had decided to follow her sister to Colombia. In late May 2018, she gave us her four-week notice. We had no one to take over for her. I don't think Mamá realized right away what this meant, or even acknowledged that it was really happening, that Luz meant it, and that the clock was ticking. She refused to talk about it. I insisted, kept circling back to the topic, but my mother ignored me, tried brushing it off. "We'll see," she said. "I'll do my best," she repeated, which made me furious. Those words meant absolutely nothing; Mamá couldn't do anything on her own. Saying "I'll do what I can" was her way of avoiding a problem that would just end up in my hands. Luis didn't have answers, Andrés did nothing but complain and criticize, and all my mother would say was that she'd do her best. I felt like no one was trying to find a solution, and that when they responded with disinterest, they were letting all the weight fall on my shoulders, even though I didn't know what to do. It felt unfair. I was the daughter, the kid sister. Why was I the one who had to deal with it all? Sometimes I fantasized about dying and watching things unfold in my absence from some vague location in the afterlife.

I ended up regretting every word that came out of my mouth. In our phone calls, there was far too much crying and yelling, too much we wished we hadn't said. But Mamá and I always made up. She'd say she understood where I was coming from but didn't know what to do, and I'd say the same thing back.

Soon after Luz gave her notice, someone stole the internet cables from Mamá's house again. The only way to get back online was to bribe a technician, which my mother refused to do. Júlia tried to help me find a work-around, although she herself had been without internet for a year. Since the cables were frequently stolen, the few local telecom companies still in operation had started selling 3G modems people would connect to their laptops with a flash drive. But that wasn't going to solve Mamá's problem; the only devices she used were an iPad and a smartphone. I managed to keep her connected by adding minutes to her phone, but with no Wi-Fi at her disposal, she could no longer watch movies or use the apps on her iPad, which meant that she was bored, with more time on her hands to lament her situation.

The power cuts were becoming even more frequent, and since she could no longer turn on the air-conditioning in her eternal-summer city, Mamá started sleeping on the sofa in the living room, which was cooler than the bedroom. But that wasn't good for her arthritic joints, so she stopped sleeping at night and slept during the day instead, in spurts. When the power was off, the water pump didn't work either. That made it harder to cook or use the bathroom, because the water had to be fetched by bucket, something Mamá couldn't do on her own. After Luz left in June, Júlia and my aunt stopped by every now and then to help out, but my mother's quality of life plummeted. Though we tried hiring a couple of women to come by and do work, they didn't meet Mamá's standards. For years, Luz had not only cared for Mamá but also done the cleaning, shopping, and cooking. It'd been no small feat. She was irreplaceable.

Those weeks were nebulous and difficult. We improvised day in and day out, just to get basic things done. In August I flew to Maracaibo. Luis sent a friend to collect me at the unair-conditioned airport, which felt like a sauna. The hall was suffocating and dimly lit, a snapshot of the aftermath of multiple blackouts. "We've been running on generators for months," an employee told me. Two days before my arrival, Maduro had announced that in September he was going to increase the monthly minimum wage from 5.2 million bolívares (equal to $0.56 USD according to the parallel exchange rate) to 180 million bolívares ($19.56 USD). At the time, the increase made it possible for a worker who had been able to buy just a quarter kilo of cheese a month to buy half a kilo of cheese plus two kilos of flour, two kilos of meat, half a kilo of ham, one can of tomato sauce, and a few vegetables. But this temporary fix was a continuation of the government's disastrous economic decisions. The IMF had already predicted that Venezuela's inflation rate, which was verging on the five digits, could reach 1,000,000 percent by the end of the year.

The country was also in the midst of a currency reconversion. In March, the government had anticipated cutting three zeros from the depleted currency, but at the last minute they decided instead to strike five zeros from the bolívar fuerte, which had been in circulation since 2007, when Chávez reduced the number of zeros to disguise the currency's devaluation. Given that hard cash was already scarce, the actual hard part now was doing the math: 100,000 bolívares fuertes turned into one bolívar soberano under the currency reconversion, which was more of a face-lift than a real economic policy. The equivalencies didn't make sense; subtracting five zeros was harder than it seemed.

The streets of my middle-class neighborhood were more deserted than ever. At first, I thought it might be because of a strike called by opposition leaders, but then I realized that in Venezuela's stagnant economy, the impact of a strike was negligible and bore no comparison to the blows Chávez was dealt in 2002. The country was in a permanent state of strike. With the exception of the lines at the gas station, Maracaibo looked like the setting of a postapocalyptic film. There was trash piled on the corners and a handful of old, patched-up cars rolling down the streets. It was almost completely silent. There was no one on the sidewalks rushing to school or to work, or walking their dogs, and there were no open stores.

When I got home, my mother seemed thinner, as if somehow her wheelchair made her look smaller. She gently raised her arms, which were more delicate than ever, and hugged me. As I unpacked the food I'd brought, my frustration and rage about the whole situation reached a boiling point. I sat on the floor to change the wheels on her wheelchair. Buying them had taken another international operation. For months,

Mamá had been asking me to replace the worn rubber wheels, but they were impossible to track down in Venezuela. Eventually, I managed to get some from an e-retailer in the United States and had them sent to a friend in California who was going to Caracas soon. But there was no safe way for her to get them to Maracaibo, and I was scared they'd be stolen in the mail. So I asked her to mail them to another friend in Miami, who would take them to the airport, where I was stopping for a three-hour layover on my way to Maracaibo.

Not long before that, I'd renewed my mother's medical insurance, with the caveat that it was worthless. Because of the crisis, there was no way for the cost of any plan to remain stable. It was impossible to predict inflation or currency devaluation, so insurance companies could only offer to maintain their contracts at a low cost "in order to keep up the relationship, in case things go back to normal one day," the broker told me, urging me to renew Mamá's. If the country managed to finally clean itself up, they wouldn't be able to get my mother on new insurance. So I renewed it; he had convinced me.

"Things can't go on like this, Mamá. You can't keep living here," I said, setting off the fight that had been simmering for years. "I'm not leaving my home," she said. "I'll do my best."

It's hard. You spend your whole life building a home, buying things you like or that feel essential, decorating your living spaces. Then comes the day when you can no longer take care of them. It's like this under normal circumstances too, but there was nothing normal about our situation. I couldn't remember how many times I'd painted those walls and fences, or waterproofed the roof with the silver coating you can only apply during mornings or late afternoons, to avoid the blinding reflection of the sun. I had bought almost every appliance in that house.

I was convinced that my mother needed to move in with one of her sisters in San Cristóbal. That way she'd have company and someone to help her day to day. At least that's what I thought—Andrés criticized my suggestion but offered no other solutions, and then made matters worse by calling frequently to harass and insult me. I understood why our mother didn't want to leave her house. I wouldn't want to leave mine either. But we didn't have a choice. I didn't want her to be alone in Maracaibo after I left, which is why I insisted she live temporarily with her sister in San Cristóbal, who agreed to the plan. After a lot of back-and-forth, Mamá reluctantly conceded, and we started packing up.

Chapter 13

You Can't Go Back

In the past few years, I've said a lot of goodbyes to people, places, jobs, and belongings, but it never gets easier. The distance has only made me feel more attached. In 2018, as the situation in my hometown grew untenable, walking away from my childhood house was harder than it was the previous times, even though it'd been fifteen years since I lived there and eight since I left the country.

As I locked the two outer gates—you can never have too many gates in Venezuela—I gazed at the terra-cotta floor that Mamá had made my brothers and me wax three times a week, then at the concrete pergola she'd installed to keep the house cool because the Maracaibo heat was at odds with all that cement.

I know every brick in that house where I grew up, every one of the added structures that ended up turning it into a bunker after two decades of trying security bars and various other strategies to protect it, and us, from the deepening violence and instability.

While I packed up the kilos of food I'd brought to her from Brazil or shipped to her over several months to stave off the shortages, Mamá stayed in bed, her back to me. Even though she'd agreed to the move, at the end of the day, it was mostly my decision.

I hired a car to drive us to San Cristóbal. Because of the scarcity of gas, transportation was now a special industry. Filling a forty-liter tank cost less than 50 bolívares fuertes, a currency still circulating during that period of transition ($0.000005 USD at the parallel exchange rate), but because of the cash shortage, gas station attendants in Maracaibo only accepted 1,000 bolívar-fuerte bills ($0.00010 USD). Fuel was sold not only at the pump but also by the gallon, for US dollars. Maduro talked about hiking the price of gas again, but his proposal, which promised to bring the price of oil in Venezuela to parity with other countries, seemed impractical in a place where the monthly minimum wage, after a 4,000 percent increase, was still only $19.56 USD. Maduro then vowed to give subsidies to anyone who got fingerprinted and presented their homeland card, which my mother still hadn't applied for. One of my cousins, who had also refused to apply for a homeland card, finally succumbed; resisting was a luxury she couldn't afford when she had a car that ran on gas.

Living in Venezuela was like a permanent act of submission, and it wasn't because people didn't have principles or weren't fed up, but because they were busy trying to survive. This submission—inevitable for those who face the constant challenges of living there—was visible all over. In the empty grocery stores, in the butcher shops protected by the National Guard, in the dimly lit banks turned into concrete ovens by the high temperatures, and in the hospitals empty of doctors and medical supplies. At the endlessly crowded bank branches with long lines snaking out from their ATMs, people's feelings of submission mixed with frustration. The daily ATM withdrawal limit at the time was 10 bolívares soberanos (1,000,000 bolívares fuertes), which is why people stood in line for hours to see a teller so they could withdraw 50 bolívares soberanos—but that wasn't even enough to buy a kilo of precooked corn flour on the black market.

In making the final preparations for our trip, I strolled down Avenida Cinco de Julio, where growing up I'd watched the Carnaval parade, ogled Christmas decorations, walked to school, and wandered with my father in the afternoons to buy bread from his friend's bakery. All I could see now were empty buildings and, in cases like the bakery, the ruins of businesses that were prosperous when I was young. The bookstore I'd gone to throughout college was still there—though it now mostly sold knickknacks—as was the confectioner's where on Sundays Papá would buy each of us a pastry, a coveted weekend treat. There were thirty people standing in line outside. The store still sold traditional desserts like galletas de huevo, but to stay in business, they'd relinquished part of their space to sell bread and deli meats, among other things. I asked a woman what she was going to get, and she answered with a simple: "Whatever's in stock." "Cheese? Bread? Eggs? Anything in particular?" I insisted. "I don't know, we'll see. Whatever's in stock." I went to the entrance and an employee there told me all they had was bread and soda; they'd run out of cheese.

The avenue's traffic lights were off. In another time, they'd been a model of modernity and synchronization. Now the cars crossing the avenue looked like they were part of a Tetris game in which everyone rolled into the intersection at the same time but somehow never crashed into each other. There wasn't much traffic, though, and a lot of the street was taken up with tanker trucks that sold water to compensate for the regular shortages in that infernal city.

I tried to get my mother excited about the move. The weather was better. She'd have company. But it was pointless.

On that Sunday in August, we got in the car that would take us to San Cristóbal, the city where she'd grown up, and I was surprised to find her smiling—and myself crying. It was incredibly hard to shut the gate and say goodbye to the plants my mother had taken such care to cultivate, giving life to that desolate setting. I'd grown up there, and I'd always come back. Now, I had no idea if I'd ever set foot in that place again. I also didn't know whether I was doing the right thing. I was convinced the move was necessary; Mamá couldn't keep living alone on a ghost street, at the mercy of criminals and cut off from vital services. All the same, moving felt a bit like giving in, and the uncertainty made this seem like a definitive goodbye to my childhood and my city, to the terra-cotta floor and the walls my father and I used to paint every Christmas.

In decades past, we used to drive from Maracaibo to San Cristóbal, the city tucked in the Venezuelan Andes, where my mother lived until the age of twenty. The two cities are separated by a mere 450 kilometers that run along the Colombian border. The biggest challenge of our trip this time would be fueling up, since the majority of gas stations on that route were closed for most of the week by decree, as the government thought this was the best way to combat contraband. Gas was highly sought after and being illegally sold for Colombian pesos, with the National Guard's explicit consent, which is how everything was done in that region. What little could be bought with bolívares was too expensive for a Venezuelan earning minimum wage. Not wanting to fuel up on the road, the driver I'd hired stuck a couple of gallons of gas in his trunk. We drove by a dozen military posts along the way, all of them bearing the face of Chávez, who despite having died five years earlier was still featured in official propaganda and on government buildings, like some kind of mystical head of the chain of command.

I hadn't been to Mamá's hometown in a decade, but as we made our way down winding roads, I started recognizing places from my past—like the site of a gas station restaurant where my brother Luis waited for me, sitting on the hood of his car, arms crossed and laughing, because it was my first time driving on those truck-filled roads and I hadn't managed to keep up with him. There was no more restaurant, no gas station, no brother, no cars, no laughter—just abandoned buildings.

When we got to the city, forty kilometers from the Colombian border, the first thing we saw was a huge line of cars at a gas station. Unlike Maracaibo, San Cristóbal didn't get much gas from the government, which led to long queues waiting for the pumps to open. The cars were numbered, and the entire process was overseen by the National Guard, who'd place a traffic cone on the ground behind the last car to be fueled. Hell was arriving at a line just to see that the cone had already been set down.

We got to the house where my aunt Margarita—whom everyone called Marga—lived. My cousin, the only one of four siblings who hadn't left the country, and who also had two kids living abroad, told me she needed to sleep for a couple of hours because she'd been in line to get gas when the pumps opened at 4:00 a.m. Tía Marga, one of Mamá's three sisters who were still faithful to the revolution, was listening to Maduro on the TV. My mother rolled her eyes, and I knew things weren't going to be easy.

San Cristóbal was in better shape than Maracaibo, though they had the same problems. There was trash all over, and a short supply of buses and taxis meant people walked for hours to and from work in a city of steep hills—a detail that, once again, made it hard to hire someone to help Mamá. There were also power cuts, though you felt it less in the Andes, where it was never hotter than 80 degrees Fahrenheit. Phone and internet service dropped so often that when people paid for something by card at a shop, they read out their PINs so the cashier wouldn't have to move the machine and risk losing the signal. The natural gas shortage was new. In the state of Táchira, most houses used gas cylinders instead of piped gas. With the crisis in the public sector, people sometimes went weeks without the gas they needed to cook food, which led to a steady stream of protests and street blockades.

Tía Marga listened religiously to the state news station, which painted a picture of a very different Venezuela: one filled with happy people whose basic needs were met by an all-powerful government that provided school materials, food, medication, and even clothes for everyone around the country. A Venezuela that no citizen ever left. A country that hundreds of people flocked back to after being mistreated in other countries, because life was better here, without a doubt. The newscast sounded like a mishmash of phrases pulled from Chávez's speeches, and even though it tried to frame Maduro and his cabinet's appearances positively, all it ended up doing was making the country sound like a place where the only real events were senior officials giving people things. The president was the star of the show, and was often featured announcing additional bonuses and subsidies for anyone with a homeland card.

My aunt's neighborhood spoke of a different reality, of course. There was news going around that a supermarket manager had been arrested after an audit found they were overcharging for products, but everyone was far more interested in the news that meat was going to be delivered that afternoon. Venezuela seemed constantly on edge. Queues had a Pavlovian effect on citizens, who'd see more than ten people milling around a storefront and immediately want to know what they were selling. It was easy to slip into this logic, even when you had food at home. The anxiety produced by the shortages was hard to control.

The supermarkets were crawling with police officers, the butcher shops with soldiers, all there to make sure the outdated price controls were being enforced. Informal vendors on street corners played hide-and-seek with them. Some didn't even have a stall; they just wandered around with their products and sold them to anyone who asked. My aunts and cousins worked around the clock to track down provisions. They never stopped. Most of them bought from informal vendors, and nearly all of them had relatives sending money from abroad. They went back and forth from Colombia to buy food and exchange money. "I get sad every time I have to cross that bridge; it's like we're at war. I only go because I have no other choice," one of my cousins told me while walking toward the bridge, pushing a shopping cart. The national flag, sun bleached and shredded, wavered at one end of the bridge, meters before the first Colombian boundary post. Hundreds of Venezuelans stood at marked lines, waiting to file through the various passport control points. When someone was sent back because their passport or migration card wasn't stamped, all they had to do was look around and a coyote would pop up with a solution.

I managed to track down an aide for Mamá in my aunt's neighborhood, which meant she could come by every day. We negotiated a salary in secret because my aunt didn't agree with her terms. I told the woman to deal directly with me and not to do any other work in the house but care for my mother. I thanked my aunt for taking Mamá in and told her that it was temporary, that we'd find a solution. "Don't worry about it, mija. She's my sister and there'll be a place for her here as long as I'm alive," she reassured me.

The day before I left to go back to Brazil was my mother's birthday. But we were so far from the times when, during family gatherings at one house or another, the whiskey would flow and there'd be large pots of food. In this Venezuela, we bartered for the birthday cake and raised glasses of sangria instead of champagne, though a dozen beers showed up courtesy of my uncle. We spent the evening talking about the past, about the lives we no longer had and weren't sure we'd ever get back. Another cousin, who had two of her three children living abroad, toasted to a future when the family would be able to come together again at the kinds of parties they had thrown years ago.

I felt downcast leaving San Cristóbal at the break of dawn to go back to Maracaibo for my flight. I knew Mamá's arrangement was precarious, yet I chose to believe she would feel better with her sister than on her own in Maracaibo. The fact that she'd have help from Clara, the woman I'd hired, also made me feel more at ease. But it was still difficult to say goodbye. My mother made me take a slice of her birthday cake to eat on the trip, then kissed me and wished me safe travels. My taxi was stopped at more than ten checkpoints on the road to Maracaibo. At one of them, I was made to undress in a small room and a National Guard officer checked my underwear, searching me for god only knows what. I still made it to the airport in time to catch my flight.

During her first few days in San Cristóbal, my mother sounded happier than usual when we spoke on the phone. She said she was spending quality time with her sisters, especially Tía Elena, who was the most active of the three despite her eighty years of age. I couldn't believe we'd finally found a solution. Clara looked after her, bathed her, fed her, and took her out to get some sun. Mamá got to talk with her sisters, and even Tía Marga's daughter, who hadn't been in favor of my mother living with them, sounded relaxed, at least according to the first few messages Mamá sent me after I left. She was in such high spirits that she decided to go back to physical therapy, which Tía Elena helped her do.

But the happiness was short lived. Mamá started writing to me in the dead of night, saying she couldn't sleep. One afternoon in October, out of the blue, she wrote to say she'd have to go back to Maracaibo, that my aunt had given her an ultimatum. I didn't understand what was happening, so I asked if they'd gotten into a fight, but she said they hadn't. She just needed to leave. She also mentioned that Tía Marga was upset with me for not calling her and that she was making Clara do things that weren't her responsibility. Mamá unilaterally informed me that she'd be moving back to Maracaibo with Clara and had already asked my brothers for money, wanting to keep me from finding out about the plan. I tried to make her see that Clara couldn't just move on a whim to a city where she didn't know anyone. But my mother wasn't listening, and the whole situation led to even more arguments. As a compromise, I offered to find her a small rental I could pay for in dollars where she'd live temporarily with Clara. She agreed to talk to a real estate agent. In the meantime, Clara fell ill and took a few days off. What I didn't know was that when Clara was gone, Mamá didn't eat, and the reason she didn't eat was that Tía Marga would complain about the expenses, even though I'd done a large grocery run before leaving and we contributed money for the shopping. Mamá told me these things only because she was in a particularly bad place one day: my aunt had gone out and left her locked in the house on her own. I asked a cousin to pick Mamá up and take her to the doctor for me, but she didn't have the keys to the front gate; they had to wait for Tía Marga to come home. Mamá hadn't eaten much at all in days, which further weakened her already-fragile body. So when Clara came back from medical leave, we decided to move Mamá in with Tía Elena, who had a spare room. Mamá was fragile, and Tía Elena's house was farther from where Clara lived, so I asked Clara to stay full-time there, just for the first few weeks.

But Mamá was never the same again after spending almost three months at Tía Marga's. She started writing and calling more in the middle of the night. Tía Elena had taken her in with the same generosity she'd shown throughout the years, though she also had a firm, motherly hand: "Paula, you're spoiling her rotten," she'd tell me on the phone. We started talking every day, because I had the sense Mamá was feeling poorly, listless. Her messages had become unintelligible, riddled with errors.

Mamá went to see several doctors with Clara and Tía Elena, but her improvement was negligible. She didn't sleep at night. She called to tell me that she was seeing dead people in her room—that she didn't want to go to bed or even be there at all, that she could see shadows slipping in behind her when she wheeled herself to the living room. It was like that every night, my aunt said. I called Luis in tears in the middle of the night because I didn't know what else to do. He listened in silence. I guess that was his way of trying to console me.

Though my mother had her good days, she was starting to talk more and more about the dead. "I don't want to lose control. I need help," I heard her say to Tía Elena one day, in a voice message she accidentally left me.

Tía Elena, whose faith in God was infinite, promised to call the parish priest. I told her to call a neurologist instead. But it was hard to get hold of any doctor, much less a specialist. Tía Elena brought the priest home. "She doesn't have faith," he determined after speaking with Mamá. This came as no surprise; my mother was never a woman of faith, though she did embrace Catholicism, praying at home every now and then. By late November I was talking more to Clara than I was to my mother, who was always indisposed. Tía Elena refused to accept money for food, which had become a traumatic issue after what happened with Tía Marga. She'd just say, "We'll work it out later, mija." I'd deposit money in her account twice a day so she could pay for Mamá's medication and medical bills, which were piling up. One of my cousins, who lived on the second floor of the same house, helped us get her the treatment she needed.

I didn't even have time to think about tomorrow, much less the holidays, but when Clara and I worked out her end-of-year schedule, when she'd be taking a few weeks off to be with family, I called Tía Elena right away, promising to find someone to cover for Clara if she'd let Mamá stay. I asked for last-minute permission at work, and bought a plane ticket to arrive in San Cristóbal one week later, just before Clara's departure.

The first weekend of December, Mamá sounded worse than ever on the phone. She wasn't taking her medication properly, wouldn't eat, and couldn't sleep at night. She was still haunted by the dead. I thought of myself as a rational person, and chalked it all up to mental exhaustion from the insomnia. But then we fought and I realized I had no rationality left; I just wanted my mother back. It felt like she was slipping away from me. I'd promised myself that I wouldn't replicate her patterns, and yet there I was showing my concern the same way she had when I was a kid: by scolding her. Maybe it's true that in the end, all daughters turn into their mothers.

A lot of time had passed. I could no longer recall how we'd gotten here.

It wasn't just that I didn't remember—I didn't have time to think about it. All I had it in me to do was respond to each day's problems. By November 2018, I couldn't recall when my relationship with Andrés soured again, or at what point Luis, sick of his fights with Andrés, found someplace else to live in Santiago, leaving them each to their own devices. I couldn't remember exactly when Mamá became fixated on dead people, or at what point we stopped having coherent conversations—or when Clara, someone I'd met just a few months earlier, became the person I spoke to every day about deposits, medication, transfers, and hospitals. I had no idea when my house and office in São Paulo filled with Post-its with bank account numbers and reminders of things to do in Venezuela. I couldn't remember when I last told Mamá I loved her, something I'd resolved to do every day after Papá died. My life had become a succession of events without a script, and I was improvising on the fly.

I had a good job as a correspondent that I enjoyed and that allowed me to live comfortably, and I had my friends, who had become my chosen family. But I was overwhelmed, and even though I faked it on the outside—Mamá had taught me that emotions should be processed internally—on the inside I went from sadness to hopelessness to deep frustration. I told Tía Elena again and again that I didn't know what to do, because I really didn't.

That first Sunday of December, Mamá and I talked on the phone for about an hour. She wouldn't stop saying that Tía Elena and I had tricked her, accusing us of conspiring against her. She said Elena was moving the furniture around to confuse her, and that at night, dead people would appear by the wooden posts at the foot of her bed. My mother had been sick for decades, but her limitations had always been physical, never mental. She'd never been scared of dead people—that wasn't Mamá. When it came to tackling logistical issues, I could be the adult in the room, but the invisible force taking Mamá away from me made me feel like I was five years old again. We cried, shouted, pointed fingers.

On Monday, December 3, my mother seemed calmer, but early on Tuesday, when I called to say hi, I couldn't make out a single word she said. From her tone it sounded like she thought she was being coherent, but I couldn't make heads or tails of what she was saying; it was all just noise. Suspecting she'd had a stroke, I asked Tía Elena to take Mamá to the doctor right away. I also asked Luis to call her, stupidly hoping she'd perk up if she heard his voice. A few minutes later, he called me back. "You have to go to her," he told me, nonplussed. It was the same tone of voice I'd heard twenty-five years earlier, when he tried to hide his fear as we walked to the hospital where Papá was in the ICU. I told him I was going there next week to stand in for Clara while she was on vacation.

Tía Elena and Clara took my mother to the doctor, and I spoke to him on the phone. He corroborated my suspicions: it might've been a stroke—she'd need some tests and a CT scan. They took her to another clinic while I deposited money in the bank and made payments. I had to sign into my account multiple times because a new government resolution had made it difficult to access Venezuelan bank accounts from a foreign IP address. Finally my cousin lent me the money to pay the remainder, but then my aunt said Mamá wouldn't be able to have the scan until the next day, because the only place with working equipment was already closed.

Mamá hadn't said an intelligible sentence all day, but in the afternoon she asked Clara to call because she wanted to talk to me. Surprised by her sudden clarity, Clara rang me. I was walking home and on the phone with someone else. I only saw the missed call half an hour later, as I stepped into my apartment. "Mamá," I texted her, but she didn't respond, so I called.

For years, I'd been convinced the phone would ring one night only for a voice to tell me "something" had happened. But in the end, it wasn't like that. I'd been on the phone with Clara for a couple of minutes when I heard Alberto, Tía Elena's ex-boyfriend, say my mother's name. I felt my heart start beating faster. "Paula," Alberto said a second time. There was a scream from Tía Elena, and then I was screaming too. Clara must've dropped the phone without hanging up because I could hear shouting and crying—I knew they were calling her name—but I couldn't see anything. It was like I was in some dark room filled with pain.

I hung up the phone. I wanted to turn it all off, to call Clara back and hear her say it was a false alarm, that Mamá had just passed out, everything was all right and they'd go to the doctor tomorrow as planned. I called again. Clara was sobbing and stammering. In the background, my aunt—whose son had died in her arms after being shot in the head on the sidewalk in front of their house—was wailing on the phone to her younger sister. "Your mother died," Clara stuttered through tears. She was crying for a woman she'd known for just three months.

My mother was seventy-three, the same age my father was when he died. *The ironies of life,* I could imagine her saying. Early the next morning, as I made my way to the airport to catch a flight to Colombia that a friend had arranged for me, I thought about all the things we might have said to each other.

She died just twelve days shy of the twenty-fifth anniversary of my father's death. On that Monday morning in late November 1993, I had waited with my mother, older brother, and aunts and uncles for news about Papá, who was in intensive care at one of the most expensive clinics in Maracaibo. I remember that a doctor came out and asked for Papá's immediate family to enter the room where he was. I don't remember anyone saying he'd died. But when I went in with Mamá and Luis, he was lying there with his fists closed, and even though they'd removed the tubes from his throat, the cables stuck to his chest were still attached to machines, which were making that long beeping sound, the one used in movies to signal that a life has ended.

In San Cristóbal, my mother was laid in her bed, her hands clasped over a rosary that my aunt had tucked in moments after she died, saying, "God rest her soul." Death draws people like moths to a flame; God was still gathering up Mamá's soul when the few things she owned started being claimed, as Clara would later tell me. "Your Tía Elena closed the door to the room and said you were on your way, and when you got there, you'd decide about her things," added Clara, who ended up staying by my side for three days even though she didn't have to. I didn't get how people could fight over a person's meager belongings right in front of their lifeless body. My mom had sunglasses, a purse, clothes, and medical equipment. But the most disputed items were her phone and the new iPad I had given her during my last visit. I wasn't sure if we'd always been this way, or if this is what the country had turned us into.

After speaking with Clara the night Mamá died, I called Luis in tears. "I'm going, I'm leaving work now," he exclaimed as soon as he heard the news. The only thing that could take him away from his job so suddenly was tragedy. "Breathe, mami, breathe," he said. He didn't cry. I asked Luis if he could call our brother, because for weeks Andrés had been blaming me for everything and ending every call by saying I was killing Mamá. They spoke, and a little while later, Andrés called me. I held back my tears, as though I couldn't afford to be vulnerable in front of my own brother. I quickly told him everything that had happened and said I was leaving for Venezuela early the next morning. Behind his silence—the same silence he'd slipped into as a teen while gazing at my father's coffin—I could picture his face. I wanted to hug him and be hugged back, but that would have to wait for another life. In this life, even though the same pain ran through our bodies, we were like two mutts in a dogfight using what strength we had left to stay upright, eye to eye, so that we could come to a momentary truce. *It takes physical effort,* I thought as we said goodbye.

I wanted to regain my footing, so I called Luis. We'd been talking more and more lately; with him I could let out my choked-back tears. He told me there were no direct flights to Venezuela. Just flying there and back would eat up the three days off the restaurant had given him, so he couldn't go to the funeral. I went, not knowing how or when I'd come back.

After a six-hour flight, I was in Bogotá, where I boarded another flight to Cúcuta. I must've been eight when I first set foot in that border city. Back then the bolívar was stronger than the Colombian peso, so during one of our vacations to San Cristóbal, Mamá took us to Cúcuta to buy clothes. Our last trip there together was twelve years ago, when I was twenty-five. My mother drove, even though she despised the narrow winding roads of the Andean mountains, where the highways had never been widened even after years of oil money. We stopped for a few minutes in Capacho, her hometown. I wanted to see it, but she didn't want to revisit memories of the rural upbringing and the alcoholic father she and her siblings had fled by moving to the city. Mamá could only see poverty and precarity in that green place full of very old houses.

That December afternoon, as I left the Cúcuta airport with the smallest suitcase I'd brought to Venezuela in years—it weighed less than ten kilos—I could hear her warning me not to trust anyone there: people would try to swindle me, they didn't like Venezuelans, I wouldn't even need to open my mouth for them to know I wasn't from there. It didn't matter either way, because even though I fell into an Andean accent the moment I felt the mountain breeze, I didn't have the energy to talk. I texted my cousin, who was waiting in San Cristóbal, and asked her how much a taxi to the bridge was; the taxi drivers at the airport, as in other places, charged more. So I dragged my luggage over the asphalt parking lot until I got to the exit. The sidewalk was closed for construction. My suitcase's little wheels couldn't roll over the asphalt, and for a moment I thought about turning back and getting an expensive taxi. *I'm no rich person,* I thought, feeling pressure from Mamá. So I summoned strength I didn't have, found a taxi, and put on my best Andean accent to negotiate the fare my cousin had suggested.

It worked. The taxi driver only knew I was Venezuelan because I told him. Then it was twenty minutes of "No offense, but it's a difficult situation, we're getting robbed by your countrymen," "People are going hungry over there, huh?" "I still cross over because the food is cheap, but for you guys it's expensive, right?" "I accepted your fare because I didn't realize you were a veneca, the last one I picked up stole my cell phone." I nodded on autopilot as I thought about how outraged my mother would've been to hear someone call me "veneca."

Two of my cousins were waiting for me at the bridge—although I don't know how I managed to spot them from the car. The place was a sea of people and poverty, nothing like it was when I'd been there as a teenager. What would Mamá have said? Hundreds of people seethed, some leaving Venezuela with frayed backpacks over their shoulders and worn suitcases in their hands, others returning from shopping trips loaded with carts and bags. There were people trying to earn some money by selling goods or services. It was like an open-air market of destitution. One of my cousins told me I should try to enter Venezuela without getting my passport stamped, even though the Colombian border-control officer at the airport had told me I'd have to get it stamped when I revealed that my final destination was Venezuela. "The line to get in is huge; it might be dark before you get through," my cousin told me. I slipped in without the stamp.

It was strange to walk over this bridge teeming with people far worse off than I was, people fleeing or just trying their best to get by. The same bridge we'd once crossed by car—Mamá refusing to turn on her headlights, even though it was mandated by Colombian law—had been taken over by barriers that marked entry and exit lines. The sheer number of people made border control a slow process. The Colombian authorities barely looked at the documents of those leaving the country, but anyone entering had to jump through several hoops. I saw people crossing the Táchira River below the bridge, right under the noses of border control; according to one of my cousins, the officers took a cut of the money that undocumented people paid coyotes to get them across. Leaving Venezuela meant wading through water that came up to your neck. *Just one tragedy after another,* I thought, remembering headlines about people swept away by the current while crossing the river. What I hadn't imagined was that it happened in broad daylight, and no one seemed to care.

Over in San Antonio, we got into the car and started winding down into San Cristóbal. I watched Capacho roll by, trying to keep up with what my cousins were saying about how bad things had gotten. In my mind, I was reliving the times Mamá and I had driven down the same route, back when she could walk and her jet-black hair fell just past her shoulders. In those days, the mountains hadn't been falling to pieces, the potholes hadn't grown as wide as the highway, and there weren't endless National Guard checkpoints with officers whose hyena eyes probed the insides of all the cars they flagged down.

By the time we got to San Cristóbal, night had fallen. I asked to go to the funeral home straight away; I'd been traveling for almost twenty-four hours, and all I wanted to do was see my mother. Mamá had hated wakes. I hated them too. But a wake was where we would be meeting again.

The funeral home was a low-slung house. There was one main room right off the front door, which was covered in security bars. I saw my cousins and aunts sitting on the chairs lined up against the walls. In the middle was a small coffin that looked like it was meant for a child. Simple floral arrangements decorated its four corners. The coffin was open, and as I walked toward it, Tía Elena came up and hugged me. All I could do was cry. "Paulina was tired," she said.

Approaching the coffin, I traveled back twenty-five years to the Monday of my father's wake. When I saw Papá's face behind the glass that day in Maracaibo, I remember thinking that even though I'd loved him so much, at least it wasn't Mamá.

When I reached the small rust-colored coffin and saw my mother's face, I felt an emptiness that was probably the understanding that I was well and truly alone. She was in a dress my cousin had chosen. It was black and blue; I'd gotten it for her as a gift a few years before. Her face was serene in the way of the dead, who no longer feel joy but also no longer feel pain. She had on makeup and a light pink lipstick. My mother had almost never worn lipstick, and in the last few decades of her life, I was always the one who made her up, and only sporadically. I don't know why the light pink on her lips was so jarring. "She looks so pretty," Tía Elena said. Only then did I realize she was still holding me.

They'd had to make some decisions on my behalf, my cousins explained apologetically. But the truth was that I had made so many decisions in the last few years, I was relieved someone else could make these for me.

Maybe this was the same weariness Mamá had felt twenty-five years earlier when, after burying Papá, she told me I should get ready to take the reins, because she was tired. That time, Mamá had decided everything, from the white shirt and dark pants they dressed him in, to the cemetery where he was buried, Sagrado Corazón de Jesús.

Andrés phoned every once in a while to ask for a death certificate so he could take three days off from work and get a cash bonus. He also wanted photos of Mamá at the wake, which I refused to take because I didn't want those images on my phone. Luis, on the other hand, became my outlet. He was there for me as much as he could be from a distance. I felt vividly that I couldn't do it alone. Luis said Mamá had wanted to be cremated, but all I could remember was her saying over and over that she wanted her body to be donated to science so they could find a cure for her illness. In any case, rustling up a plot in a cemetery, the way we'd done for Papá a quarter of a century earlier, just wasn't possible anymore. In this new Venezuela, even dying was a problem.

I learned that things are much harder when a person dies at home. My mother had passed after dinner, seated in her red wheelchair. It was nighttime, which meant there was no way for the family to get a death certificate immediately. What little still worked in Venezuela only did so by day, so they negotiated with the only funeral home willing to take her body without a certificate. My mother's older sister, the one who looked most like her, had died in her house that same year, just a few blocks from Tía Elena's. My cousins had watched their mother start decomposing in her bed due to bureaucratic delays, so they knew they had to act quickly. They paid the funeral home, which would also be handling the cremation at the cemetery, then went first thing in the morning to ask Mamá's last doctor to sign the death certificate. At first he refused, since he hadn't seen her body. But this was the only way for them to get the document, so my cousins finally convinced him to sign a paper saying my mother had died of "cardiorespiratory failure" at 7:45 p.m. on December 4, 2018. The time was registered by my family, but the cause was poetic license. It was not their fault, of course, and Mamá would've applauded their determination, I'm sure of it. I was grateful to them, but also somewhat hurt that I'd never know what my mother's cause of death really was. All I knew from Alberto was that she had asked to speak with me after dinner, and a few minutes later, while I was on the phone with the person right next to her, she silently lifted her hand to her chest and closed her eyes, then her head fell to one side. I wondered, uselessly, what she might've been feeling or thinking. The thought that Mamá had died so suddenly that she wouldn't have had time to be afraid was a comfort. Still, I was tormented by the fact that I hadn't been there to tell her I loved her.

"Delirium," a traumatologist I visited in São Paulo a few months later told me after I described my mother's last days, searching in vain for an answer. "With older people, certain infections can sometimes cause delirium, but there's no way of really knowing," he said.

The main room of the funeral home was blue—designed to soothe mourners, I assumed, though to me it seemed cold. "Nice room, isn't it?" I heard a cousin say. *What a horrible place,* I heard Mamá respond, knowing she would've been annoyed to see where she'd been put. *What a mediocre funeral, what tasteless coffee, all those spelling mistakes in the obituary. What a contrast with your father's funeral,* she grumbled in my head. It was true—Papá's funeral was something else. The perfectly white hall was full to bursting with enormous garlands that had shown up out of the blue, and the wooden coffin sat huge and shining in the middle of a smaller, more intimate room. The ironies of life: both wakes had cost 40,000 bolívares, except Mamá's was paid for not with bolívares but with bolívares soberanos, whose zeros proliferated even as the government tried to slash them. I reimbursed my cousin with a $74 transfer, the equivalent to 39,960 bolívares at the time. For my father's funeral in 1993, my mother had to negotiate four installments that each accounted for practically her entire pension. "Look how stable our economy is—twenty-five years later, a funeral costs the same," my cousin said with a smile, and we all laughed.

As I admired Mamá's round face—free of wrinkles except for the ones on her forehead, which she only ever relaxed when I reminded her to—someone handed me a phone with Tía Elisa on the line. She was in Maracaibo and hadn't been able to come. She expressed her condolences, then proceeded to say that my mother had promised her a cell phone—could I make sure to send it? I heard Mamá's voice in my head one more time: *I told you your aunt only cares about herself.* I had to give it to Mamá again; I'd had such a hard time accepting that she was right about this, and now it was happening to me. To appease my aunt and her anxiety over the cell phone, I told her I hadn't been aware of this, but that she could take whatever food was still in the house in Maracaibo, the stuff I hadn't been able to bring to San Cristóbal. Later,

I found out that Tía Elisa hadn't even waited for Mamá to be cremated; she looted her own sister's house the next day. I'd stuck up for Elisa countless times whenever Mamá was cross with her, only to wind up railing against her, tearfully declaring that I wanted nothing to do with her ever again. I was still obsessing about it a couple of months later when Luis told me, "You've got to understand. People lose their heads when they're hungry and in need. Try and forget about it."

That night after the wake, we were asked to leave the funeral home because the streets were empty and it was dangerous to be anywhere but home. When Papá died, I kept vigil at the funeral home all night. I wouldn't be able to do the same for Mamá. Funeral homes no longer operated around the clock. Though they might have agreed to let me stay, Tía Elena said we'd be safer at her house. There was a single security gate at the funeral home entrance, and it looked especially vulnerable.

The first thing I saw at my aunt's house was the wheelchair we'd gone to such lengths to get, although Mamá barely had time to use it. An empty wheelchair can be such a painful thing to look at. The family talked about how much I'd helped Mamá—with her medication, medical equipment, iPad, cell phone, sunglasses, clothes, doctor appointments. About how expensive the wheelchair must've been and how much food was still left of what I'd shipped to her or brought to her myself. But all I saw was a pile of junk: an empty wheelchair, a cell phone she'd never again speak into, medication that could no longer soothe her pain. I listened to them in silence. Tía Elena, Clara, and my cousins may not know this, but they propped me up in those hours, as I went from feeling indifference to rage at Venezuela.

Clara slept by my side that night. My aunt didn't like it, but we slept in the same bed where my mother had spent the last few nights before she died. I saw the bedposts—the ones Mamá had described in her predawn phone calls about the dead—and thought, *Well, Mamá, here I am wishing I could see the dead, but they're just wooden posts. I told you there was nothing there, you have to give me that.*

Someone had left a candle and a glass of water on the nightstand for the souls in purgatory, just as my mother had done twenty-five years earlier, at her most devout, for my father. By candlelight, Clara told me in whispers about how Tía Marga had begrudged Mamá her food, measuring out every spoonful of flour or rice, and complained about how I never bought anything for the house. Mamá never mentioned that their relationship soured because nothing was enough for my aunt—at the end of the day, my salary was in dollars, and that's all that mattered. Mamá also never mentioned that she'd retaliated against her sister's stinginess by refusing to eat, which only served to exacerbate her poor health. That was why she ended up in the emergency room one weekend, accompanied by my cousin Sandra.

I asked Clara to stop there. Just as it hurt me to think of my father in a concentration camp, it broke my heart to think of how my mother had suffered at the hands of her own sister. But unlike what Papá had lived through, the adversity Mamá faced was my fault. She'd told me she never wanted to leave her house, and Tía Marga had quickly shown her true colors. Her daughter had chastised me for moving my mother into their home. Despite all that, I left her there. *I didn't know what else to do, Mamá,* I thought in a futile apology.

Most of my family showed up at the funeral home the next day, including Tía Marga and her daughter. I was given a choice of three boxes for my mother's ashes. They were all huge and ugly. One was a replica of the plain coffin where she lay. Mamá hated replicas, so I chose a light-colored wood box, though I hesitated because it had a cross on the side. My mother hadn't been a believer, something the priest himself had confirmed. The gulf between religion and my mother was so wide, my cousins were afraid to tell me they'd paid for a mass to end the ceremony. As we made our way to the cemetery, I saw that the streets had been taken over by lines for gas. San Cristóbal was still prettier than Maracaibo, though not immune to poverty—the traffic lights weren't working because of the power cuts, and there was trash everywhere. The garbage trucks came only occasionally, and my cousins stored their trash in a freezer for days so the sidewalk wouldn't get overrun with waste. If they were at home when the truck went by, they'd run out the door with their bags of frozen scraps the moment they heard it. "A taxi driver recently offered to take all the trash from our block if we paid him. It's crazy, I know, but we might have to do it. The freezer's full and we don't know when the garbage truck will come again," Sandra told me as I calculated how much gas my being there had cost them.

When we got to the cemetery, the sun was beating down. In the Andes, the sun will burn your cheeks no matter how cold it is. We went to the main building, distant from the gardens, where cremations were handled. Minutes later, a clerk came out of the administration office with the wood box. Another clerk took my mother to another room, then asked those closest to the deceased to go inside that room to identify the body.

I wasn't familiar with the procedure, but I went in, along with Tía Elena, a cousin, and Sandra, who looked more like Mamá than I ever had. I didn't expect to see my mother lying on a platform in front of the furnace doors. They'd removed her body from the rented coffin, one of two the funeral home had. Because of the crisis, there were no new coffins available, so buying one was not an option. My cousins had chosen the other coffin—they told me this later—but the previous body had taken longer than expected to vacate it, which is why my mother had been temporarily laid to rest in the rust-colored child-sized one. Mamá would've been outraged. She had no shoes on and was cold to the touch, but I found some comfort in stroking her smooth black hair, the only part of her that still looked alive. I could see the swelling on one side of her body. She was starting to decompose.

Tía Elena took the rosary from Mamá's hands and gave it to me. My mother looked so incredibly still. I wanted to believe that souls existed, that she really was in heaven with some god, that the rosary, which I now keep on my nightstand, was a tangible piece of her soul.

"Your mother told me something. She made me swear to keep it a secret until she died. I can tell you now, right?" Tía Elena said as we waited for the cremation to start. Before any of us had a chance to question her inability to keep secrets, she reminded us she'd kept her promise. Though we expected her to reveal some great mystery, what she told us was that my mom had tried weed when she was young, and she hated it. More than surprising us, it made us laugh that this was the secret Mamá chose to take to her grave. But it turned out she had kept secrets, as I would find out later that afternoon.

Alberto, who'd known my mother since she was a teenager, told me things about her I'd never suspected, like the fact that she was engaged to another man when she was around twenty years old. As he did, I silently asked, *Why, Mamá?* We could've talked about love and heartbreak. Instead, we spent our phone calls either criticizing each other or talking about food, medication, dollars, and transfers. Maybe our relationship could have improved in our last few years together, as I started to understand her better. I was no longer a young idealist, determined to prove that she and I were different. As an adult, I had started seeing myself in her and wasn't bothered by the resemblance. Even though I recognized some personality traits I chose not to perpetuate, other things I picked up on made me proud. But Mamá and I had never spoken about that. The country and its disasters took that from us.

A little less than two hours later, the clerk brought us the wooden box with the cross on one side. "Her ashes weigh 2.8 kilos, which is what she would've weighed when she was born, according to popular belief. They are a light gray color, which means she was a good and patient person, also according to popular belief," said the clerk as he gave me the box. I couldn't help but laugh. "I wouldn't call Mamá patient," I said by way of explanation, embarrassed to have laughed at such a somber moment—which is exactly how I'd felt twenty-five years earlier when I burst out laughing in the middle of Papá's funeral mass.

I left the cemetery with Mamá in my hands.

Clara came with me to Tía Elena's house. When we walked into the room, she told me that days earlier, Mamá had asked to see her old class ring. "It's for Carola," she'd told Clara. At home I'd never been Paula, because Mamá was Paula. Instead, I went by variations on my middle name: Caro, Carola, or Carolita to my brothers, my father, my aunts and uncles, and my mother too, of course. This always made me feel like I had a parallel life with an alter ego. I hate the name Carola. Still, whenever I hear someone call me that, I'm transported home, to my childhood, to another world, a world different from the place Paula lives in, where I'm an adult with responsibilities.

I had to decide what to do with Mamá's things because I needed to clean out her room at Tía Elena's. This reminded me of watching Mamá spend a whole afternoon silently folding the few shirts and pants Papá owned: some house clothes and a pair of blue jeans he'd bought after his seventieth birthday, in what he referred to as an attempt to get with the times. His Pino Silvestre cologne; the thick acrylic glasses; the planners containing his shopping lists for parties; the belts, which he'd used on my brothers more than once. In just a few hours, everything was boxed and ready to be taken away.

I never imagined, that afternoon long ago, that one day twenty-five years later I'd be doing the same for my mother.

I don't remember being particularly close with Tía Elena, but ever since I'd gotten to San Cristóbal, she'd treated me like a daughter—feeding me, talking to me, and taking care of me. "Mija, you have to come back to visit because your family, your home, your country live on here," she said when we got back from the cemetery. I hadn't needed to say anything for my aunt, mother of five, to sense that Venezuela and the concept of family had suddenly become abstractions now that my parents were gone and my brothers lived in Chile.

A few years earlier, I'd told Mamá that I didn't remember seeing her cry when Papá died, that from the outside his death had seemed easy for her. In those days, she became more flexible and started to watch telenovelas. Every day after lunch, Mamá would watch a Mexican one whose protagonist was an aspiring mariachi musician. I knew every song by heart. She was a fan of Pedro Infante and Mexican cinema, and she'd taught me dozens of ranchera songs starting when I was little. Even though I knew how much she loved them, I was still surprised the day Mamá started singing along, full of emotion, as the protagonist crooned "Ojalá que te vaya bonito." I can still see her sitting on the bed as if in a trance. I don't know who José Alfredo Jiménez was thinking about when he wrote that song, but I'm almost certain Mamá was thinking about Papá as she listened to it. Full of rage and sorrow at her death, I now found myself thinking about that song, too.

In hindsight, I lived those days after my mother's death as an out-of-body experience. I thought I had things under control, when in fact I was going about in a dream state, partially numb. I know I wasn't myself because one night a few months after, as I was watching TV, I snapped out of that stupor and started thinking about Mamá's favorite shawl. I rushed to my closet and sobbed tears of joy when I realized I'd held on to it. Since then, I've cried more often and felt more sorrow. It's like my body had protected itself by putting a part of me to sleep to get me through the days after her death.

The fact that a part of me was asleep and slowing me down was clear to the people around me. I could barely function. So one of my cousins took charge of getting my paperwork to leave Venezuela, and Sandra promised to drive me to the border.

That morning, we got up before dawn. Tía Elena wanted to take advantage of that car trip to buy food. When I woke up at 5:30, the coffee had already been brewed and there were arepas—round, delicate, and perfect—sizzling on the griddle. Soon Sandra and her sister came to collect us. When I asked how they'd managed to get gas without bribing someone or waiting in a line all day, they said they'd called in an emergency favor from a friend who ran a gas station. I was surprised to see that the fuel tank indicator was already at half-empty, and asked if something was wrong. "No, but if the guards stop me at the border and see the tank is full, they could arrest me for intent to sell fuel. I put half the tank in my brother's car just in case," Sandra explained, as if having to think like that was totally ordinary.

I thought about everything we'd normalized over the last decade. Without our realizing it, scraping by had become the new normal. At the end of the day, what could we do but accept it, seek out solutions, get by, and rejoice over our small victories? It was all proof that we really were surviving; that we really could keep going; that there wasn't a National Guard we couldn't outsmart, or an economic disaster that could defeat us; that, in the worst of cases, there was no government that could take away the grooving we'd already done, as we say in the Caribbean.

We parked the car and started walking to cross over to Colombia. "Let's go! Let's go!" shouted the border-control officer at the Simón Bolívar bridge as we walked in lines like ants, as quickly as the crowd would let us. "The way they humiliate us makes my blood boil every time I have to cross the border. It drives me crazy, but I keep quiet because I have no choice," my cousin said to me through gritted teeth, shopping cart rolling behind her. Though I wouldn't be making the trip back, I shared her frustration. People crossed that bridge to Colombia out of need—for food, medication, money, a new life. Some of the Colombian border-control officers and Venezuelan soldiers seemed to take a sadistic pleasure in witnessing all that despair.

That border is a small-scale reproduction of how Venezuela functions. People with documents can leave, people with no documents but enough money can pay to leave, and people with nothing are left to their fates. On the Venezuelan side, the soldiers are king. It's lawless, and they get to decide who crosses and how. Necessity is the mother of invention—new services pop up to meet any situation. That border is also where hundreds of people from a paralyzed country in ruins wander around like lost souls, waiting for something—though what that is, they cannot say.

In Cúcuta, I wanted to take my aunt and cousins out for breakfast, but getting them to accept was an uphill battle. Tía Elena, who'd fed me many times in the past when we visited her, wouldn't let me buy her coffee and an empanada. My cousins, who had taken me out on the town when I was a teenager, insisted that I mustn't throw away my money on something like that. They saw coffee and three empanadas as a luxury; I saw it as the least I could do to thank them for the love they'd shown me during the hardest days of my life.

"Come back whenever you want, mija," my aunt said, hugging me. Then I climbed into the taxi that would take me to the airport. My cousins negotiated the fare; I sat in silence the entire ride. Even though Cúcuta abutted Venezuela, it couldn't have looked more different. It was a normal city: there were people walking to work or taking a stroll, open storefronts, working traffic lights, and public transit. In the taxi I thought about how, when Andrés had taken the same roads as he left Venezuela, he'd written to say he was surprised there was no garbage in the streets.

I got to the airport early and sat down at the end of the hall to wait for my flight. I thought of what Tía Elena had said and wondered if I'd ever come back. As I waited, I thought about this and about my parents. About how Mamá had never wanted to go back to the town where her family lived. "It's not home anymore," she'd say whenever we talked about moving her to San Cristóbal. I thought about how my father had claimed that Spain was not home whenever my mother talked to him about moving to Europe. "This is my home," he'd say, meaning Venezuela. I did want to come back, but not to visit. I wanted to come back to something that didn't exist anymore.

Then I thought of the time Papá and I sat on the hood of the family car after another one of their arguments about Europe. As we gazed up at the stars, I asked if it was true that he didn't want to go back. He looked at me with those sad eyes I've spent my whole life trying not to forget, then shook his head. "Sometimes you can't go back."

ABOUT THE AUTHOR

Photo © 2022 Patrick T. Fallon

Paula Ramón is a Venezuelan journalist who has lived and worked in China, the United States, Brazil, and Uruguay. She is currently a correspondent for Agence France-Presse, based in Los Angeles. She has written and reported for the *New York Times*, *National Geographic*, *Columbia Journalism Review*, and *Piauí* magazine, among other outlets.

ABOUT THE TRANSLATORS

Photo © Dagan Farancz

Julia Sanches translates books from Portuguese, Spanish, and Catalan into English. Born in Brazil, she lives in New England.

Photo © University of Iowa

Jennifer Shyue is a translator from Brooklyn, New York.